PHONICS

a resource bank and teachers' guide

Jill Gregory

John Murray

Acknowledgements

I should like to thank the following people for their comments and suggestions, which were most useful:
Mrs J. Brown, Mrs A. Marsh, Mrs P. Lister, Mrs M. Mackean and Mr B. Gregory. I am also grateful to Mrs A. Cochrane at John Murray for her guidance and support.

First published 1982
Reprinted 1982, 1988, 1990, 1992, 1993, 1994, 1996, 1997, 2000
by John Murray (Publishers) Ltd
50 Albermarle Street, London W1X 4BD

Typeset by H. Doust Art and Advertising
Printed in Great Britain by
Athenæum Press Ltd, Gateshead, Tyne & Wear

British Library Catalouging in Publication Data

Gregory, Jill
    Phonics.
    1. Reading (Secondary education) 2. Reading
    – Remedial teaching 3. Reading disability
    4. Phonetics
    I. Title
    371,91'4   LB1 632

    ISBN 0-7195-3851-3

Contents

Worksheets

Notes for the teacher

INTRODUCTION

In 1976, as the head of the Remedial Department in a large London secondary school, I had to organise remedial work for more than seventy pupils entering the first year with varying degrees of reading disability.

The need, at that time, was for a flexible scheme of work which would motivate the pupils, could be entered at the level appropriate to each one, and which could be used by teachers who were not specially trained in remedial work. The scheme presented in this book has been amended many times and I have retained only those units which have proved successful in use.

The main objective of the whole scheme is to increase the pupils' vocabulary and to help them to acquire the necessary reading and verbal skills which will enable them to function well in the classroom. It is aimed at pupils with a reading age of between 6.0 and 10.0 years.

The scheme is based on a sequence of worksheets which teachers are invited to reproduce for class use. These are intended to be used not in isolation but in conjunction with other materials — readers, both fiction and non-fiction, spelling packs, games and work devised by the teacher. The material here will provide the basis for up to three years' work.

The worksheets are designed to stimulate discussion and some will provide themes for drama. The completed worksheets may be put together by the pupils to make a book. The pupils can then see their own progress as the book builds up and will also have material to which they can refer.

Please note that for convenience the pronoun 'he' is used to refer to teachers and pupils of both sexes.

SUPPLEMENTARY MATERIAL

The teacher can add to the enjoyment and effectiveness of the scheme in the following ways:

1   By using the five basic games, Secret Passages, Car Race, Points of the Compass, Butterfly and Castle, which can be duplicated and used with any phonic unit. Full instructions for the games are given on pp. xi-xx.

2   By constructing large playing boards for the Forest Trail, Mountaineering, Planet X and Tree games (see models on pp. 9—12). The suggested size of card for these games is 795 mm x 545 mm.

3   By gradually building up a complete set of word cards* until every listed word is on an

*Suppliers of all materials referred to are listed on p. xxiv.

individual card. These cards are essential for the large board games, and the Butterfly and Castle games. Pelmanism can also be played if two copies of each word are made.

All the games will last longer if they are mounted on boards and covered with transparent adhesive film.

NOTE: Individual word cards are best stored as a card index. A box file, with the spring removed, laid flat and sectioned off, is a cheap and effective method of storage. A guide card should separate each phonic unit from the next.

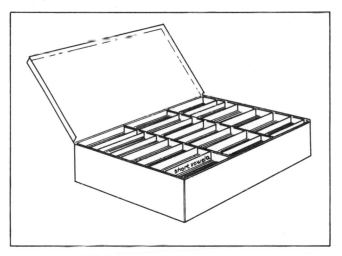

INTRODUCING THE WORK SCHEME

Initial Screening

After screening by a standardised test (some accepted tests are listed on p. xxv) pupils with similar reading ages should be placed in small groups.

There are various types of reading test such as Daniels and Diack Test 1, *The Standard Test of Reading Skill,* which is phonically based; Salford, a sentence reading test which enables pupils to make use of contextual clues; and Schonell, which is a word recognition test.

The reading age diagnosed may vary according to the test used. For example, the pupil who scores a reading age of 7.0 on the Schonell test may, if he uses contextual clues, score a slightly higher reading age on the Salford test.

The sequence below may be followed after screening with all pupils starting the scheme, whatever their reading age. Teachers may of course prefer to follow a different order.

1   The pupils complete the 'Myself' worksheet. This enables the teacher to talk informally to the group and establish a warm and friendly relationship.

2 The teacher can, at this point, introduce the pupils to the books they will be reading. If they wish to choose a book to read at home the teacher can suggest certain books at the level appropriate to their reading age (see Supplementary Reading Material p. xxi). For group reading the teacher can select sets of readers also at the appropriate reading level, and pupils can choose the set they wish to read.

3 The teacher then diagnoses the strengths and weaknesses of each pupil, using a standardised test or an informal reading inventory, that is, diagnosis of errors while the pupil reads a chosen book of an appropriate level.

An informal reading inventory

Write out a chosen passage in double spacing. The reading level should be slightly above the pupil's 'instructional' level, in order to produce a sufficient number of errors for analysis. For all but the poorest readers a minimum of 10–16 errors is necessary. Here is a suggested code for marking:

A standardised test

The object of this diagnostic testing is to find out where in the sequence of worksheets the pupil should begin. It is sometimes difficult to assess this accurately at the beginning. One test that I recommend is *The Assessment of Reading Ability* (see p. xxv). This booklet contains tests to diagnose phonic ability.

The teacher notes the weaknesses of individual pupils and finds the relevant phonic unit as a starting point in the scheme for the whole group. Teachers will find that phonic weaknesses tend to correlate with the level of attainment. A pupil with a reading age of 8.5 years should not need to learn the rules in sections A–E but may have failed to grasp many of the phonic rules in sections F–S.

Occasionally the teacher will find that one pupil in the group has already grasped a particular rule. Repeating the work on this rule will emphasise his strengths and should give him a greater sense of achievement.

Child's performance characteristics	Code	Example
Word read correctly	Tick ✓	✓ mending
Word refused	Cross through ———	~~mending~~
Word attempted only after encouragement by teacher	Underline	mending (underlined)
Word omitted	Circle ◯	he ⓘs mending
Insertion of word	∧	he is ∧ mending (not)
Word read incorrectly	Cross through ╱ Write substitution above	melting mending (crossed)
Word mispronounced	Code M Write in the mispronunciation	meending mending (M)
Child attempts phonic analysis	Write in all letters sounded in lower case interspersed with dots	m.e.n.d.i.n.g. mending
Letters sounded, then correctly blended	As above, tick at end	m.e.n.d.i.n.g. ✓ mending
Blends, digraphs or units given	Write letter groups in lower case interspersed with dots	m.end.ing mending
Letter names given	Write in capitals interspersed with dots	M.E.N.D.I.N.G. mending
Self-corrected	Write S/C ✓	meending mending S/C ✓

BASING A LESSON ON A WORKSHEET

1 The instructions are read by one or two of the group with the teacher's help, if necessary.

2 The words listed at the top of the worksheet are read, or built up, in any way the teacher chooses. Pupils may read one word in turn or, in the case of words where the rule is fairly easy to apply, say them together slowly. Although most secondary school pupils will know the meaning of all the words, one or two will not. Therefore it is a good idea to discuss the meanings.

Conversation should be encouraged. Discussing the meaning of different words and how they are used, or showing pupils pictures of some words, naturally leads to an endless variety of topics. The interchange of ideas helps the pupils to speak fluently and increase their spoken vocabulary. The length of this part of the lesson will depend on the needs of the pupils in the group.

3 A quick game can be played before starting the exercises. Here are three suggestions:

(a) As the listed words are in either four or five columns the teacher asks which pupil will be the first to say the word that is, for example, three from the top in column one, or two from the bottom in column four. Pupils count their own points. (Make sure that pupils know the meaning of the word 'column'.)

(b) Another useful two-minute game, which brings drama into the lesson and provides added interest, is the miming of various words. A pupil chooses a word to mime and says which column it is in. The other pupils have to guess the word. (Some worksheets are more appropriate for this than others.)

(c) The teacher gives each pupil in turn a word which he must find in the list and then put into a sentence which he says to the teacher.

4 The group can then do one of the following:

(a) *Complete the exercises or story on the worksheet.*
The teacher is part of the group and is there to supply any words the pupils need to know so that no frustration is experienced. The emphasis is always on the enjoyment of the reading lesson and the pleasure of success.

(b) *Play one of the games on pp. 4—12 using the words pupils are trying to learn.*
If the teacher has discussed the words at length (some worksheets need more discussion than others) he may feel that the group would benefit from playing one of the games, using the words, instead of completing the exercise.

If the teacher suspects that pupils are not sure of the meaning of some words, the games can be played with pupils putting the word into a sentence or stating its meaning.

The large board games can also be used for spelling practice. Play a game, following the instructions on pp. xvi-xx; but before the player moves his counter the pupil on his left picks up a word card and reads it to the player, who has to write it down. If he spells it correctly he gains a point which is noted by the teacher.

Each game is used to reinforce visually a unit of vocabulary and to provide the whole-word teaching approach for the small number of pupils who are unable to grasp phonic rules.

(c) *Play a game of pelmanism (pairs) using the words listed on the worksheet.*
Two sets of cards are needed for this game which is valuable for visual discrimination. As in ordinary pelmanism, the cards are placed face downwards and the pupil's aim is to acquire as many pairs as possible. The pupil chooses two cards, turns them over and reads them. If they are a pair he keeps them, if they are not, he turns them face downwards again.

(d) *Read their own choice of books (with help in selection) or read a book together.*
One of the main aims of the teacher should be to promote reading as a source of enjoyment, and pupils always feel a sense of achievement when they realise that they can apply the rules they have learnt.

SPELLING

As the ability to read a word precedes the ability to spell it a pupil's spelling age is nearly always behind his reading age. Spellings should be taught by a visuo-motor approach and teachers can explain the following method to help pupils learn their spellings:

1 *Look* at the word carefully.

2 *Cover* the word.

3 *Write* the word in one movement from memory.

4 *Check* to see if the word is correct.

5 If the word is *correct*, write it four or five times and check again to make sure that it is correct each time.

6 If the word is *incorrect*, look at the word again and find the error. Repeat the formula — look, cover, write and check — until the word has been learnt.

7 Then work through the spelling list (no more than ten words) in this way.

One method of compiling individual spelling lists is by noting misspelt words in the pupils' creative writing. This may not be easy as some older, slow-learning pupils dislike any form of writing and knowing how to motivate them in this exercise is an additional problem. One suggestion for helping pupils is to get them to write their stories and plays on prepared worksheets (see pp. 1 and 2).

The story worksheet

Teachers may like to use this worksheet in the following way:

1   The pupils are encouraged to write a story and a short time is allowed for a drawing.

2   The story is written in pencil.

3   When a pupil requires the spelling of a word the teacher supplies the word orally and the pupil writes it first in the 'spelling box' and then where he needs it in the story.

4   When the story is finished or half-finished (taking into consideration the time allotted to the activity or the interest of the pupils), the pupil reads it out to the teacher who immediately corrects any misspelt words. To do this the teacher erases the word and adds it to those in the spelling box. The pupil writes the correct word in place of the erased one. This method ensures that the completed story is not covered with alterations.

5   Before the pupil writes the spellings in his spelling book (a small memo book) the teacher may choose to add two or three words which are similar in appearance to one of those the pupil has misspelt, e.g. if the word 'could' is listed in the spelling box the teacher can add the words 'would' and 'should'.

6   When the teacher decides to end the story-writing activity all pupils transfer the spellings in the spelling box at the bottom of their story to their spelling book. They take the spellings home and learn them by the visuo-motor approach (look, cover, write, check). In a subsequent lesson the teacher tests the pupils individually while the others complete their story or drawing, or start a fresh exercise. If pupils need a follow-on page for the story this may consist of lines only with a spelling box at the bottom.

7   The play sheet may be used in the same way as the story sheet. The teacher may need to explain how to write a play. The follow-on page for the plays may include a drawing box placed in a similar position to the one on the story sheet, and a spelling box at the bottom.

8   When pupils have completed five or more stories or plays they make them into a book. The teacher can cut off the spelling box sections and file them for future reference. This provides a record of the errors each pupil is making in his creative work and of the spellings he has learnt and retained.

Spelling using the phonic units

With slower children the teacher may wish to teach groups of words that are similar in sound as well as appearance. The teacher can select, from each phonic unit, those words that pupils use most frequently in their written work. The pupils should write down the spellings in their spelling books. They can be encouraged to learn their spellings by the visuo-motor approach and in the following ways:

1   By including each spelling in a sentence.

2   By playing one of the board games (see pp. 9—12).

3   By completing a 'word search'. (This can be made up by the teacher, using words from the relevant units; see p. J4.)

SUGGESTIONS FOR HOMEWORK

The pupils may do one or more of the following:

1   Read part of a book of their own choice.

2   Read one or two chapters of the group's reading book.

3   Complete a worksheet. (The teacher may need to explain the instructions.)

4   Take a worksheet home so that they may practise the words they have learnt.

5   Learn their spellings.

USING THE CHECKLIST

The checklist (see p. 3) is invaluable as a quick guide to work covered and work still to be done. It may also be used by the pupils for their own benefit.

It is advisable for the teacher to record briefly the content of each lesson and any homework that has been given. These notes can also contain additional information, e.g. weaknesses of individual pupils.

On the checklist, reading age is abbreviated to RA and spelling age to SA.

STORING THE MASTER SHEETS

After the worksheets have been extracted from the book for duplication the teacher may find it useful to keep them in a ring binder or in an expanding file (in numerical order for easy reference). Although the duplicated worksheets can be used for further duplication they will not reproduce as clearly as the master sheet.

Preparing and using the games

The purpose of all games is to enable words which have been taught phonically to become sight words.

THE BUTTERFLY GAME

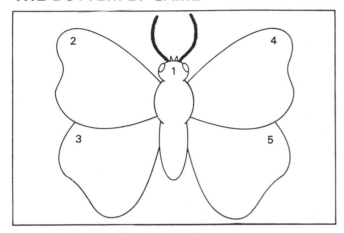

Preparation

1 Duplicate the drawing of the butterfly on p.4 (two for each pupil and one for the teacher).

2 Choose words from the phonic unit being learnt. Write, preferably in colour, a different word on each numbered part of each butterfly. If there are insufficient words in the phonic unit to fill all the numbered pieces, repeat those words which cause the most difficulty. If there are too many words, eliminate the easier words.

3 Cover the pupils' butterflies with transparent film and cut out the numbered pieces. Keep the cut out pieces in an envelope; stick the remaining whole butterfly on the front as a model.

4 Before the game starts: position the whole butterfly so that it can be seen by each member of the group. Spread out the butterfly pieces face upwards and place the pack of word cards which you have made for this unit next to them. (See Suppliers of Materials p. xxiv.)

Aim

To be the first player to complete two butterflies (the players must complete one whole butterfly before they start the second one).

Rules

1 The player whose turn it is throws the dice and picks up any butterfly piece with the corresponding number. He reads the word on that piece and on each piece he picks up as his turn comes round; and the first butterfly is gradually assembled.

2 When a player throws a six he takes a card from the top of the pack. If he can read the word on it, he may keep it and have another turn. If he cannot read the word the card must be returned to the bottom of the pack but the player still has another turn.

3 If a player throws a number he has already used in the butterfly he is putting together, he takes a card from the pack, reads it and keeps it. If the player cannot read the word, the card must be returned to the bottom of the pack.

4 When a player has accumulated five cards he may exchange them (cash them in) for whichever number he needs.

5 The winner is the first player to complete two butterflies.

THE CASTLE GAME

This is prepared and played in the same way as the Butterfly game (see p. 4).

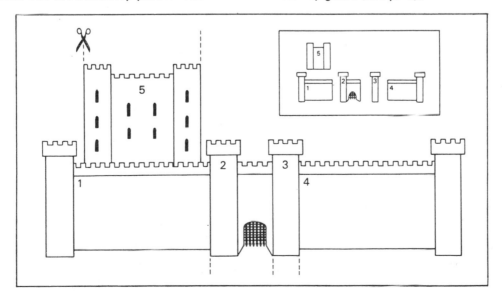

THE SECRET PASSAGES, CAR RACE AND POINTS OF THE COMPASS GAMES

Preparation (This is the same for all three games)

Make a playing board for each pupil in the group by duplicating one of the models on pp. 5—7. Select words from the phonic unit being learnt. Write, preferably in colour, a different word on each square of the playing board. If there are insufficient words in the phonic unit to fill all the squares, repeat those words which cause most difficulty. If there are too many words, eliminate the easier words.

General Rules

1 Each player throws the dice, the player who gets the highest number starts. The order of play is clockwise.

2 When a player throws a six, he takes another turn.

3 When a player lands on a penalty or bonus square he follows the instructions.

4 If a player reads a word (or words) correctly he gains a point which is noted by the teacher. The teacher may choose to help the pupil build up the word and so gain a point.

THE SECRET PASSAGES GAME

Aim (There are two winners)

1 To be the first player to arrive back in the square marked Hall.

2 To be the player who has the most points.

Rules

1 The player whose turn it is throws the dice and moves his counter the number of squares indicated by the dice. He reads the word on the square on which he has landed.

2 If a player lands on a square where a secret passage starts or finishes he follows the arrow and moves his counter upwards or downwards to another square; he reads the word on that square and on the square he has left.

3 When a player lands on a penalty or bonus square he reads the word on that square before he follows the instructions.

4 To win, a player must throw the exact number to reach the square marked Hall. If a player throws a higher number than he needs to read the Hall, he does not move but reads the word on the square that corresponds to the number on the dice, e.g. if he needs a 3 to win but throws a 5 he does not move but reads the word on square 5.

5 The points are totalled to see who has the most and is therefore the second winner.

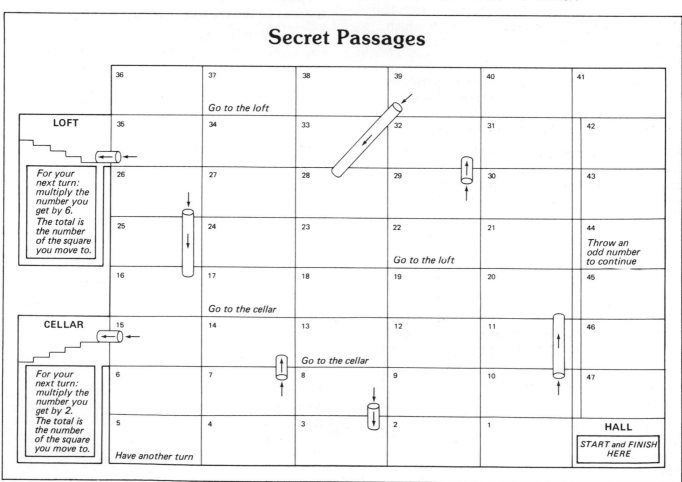

The Car Race

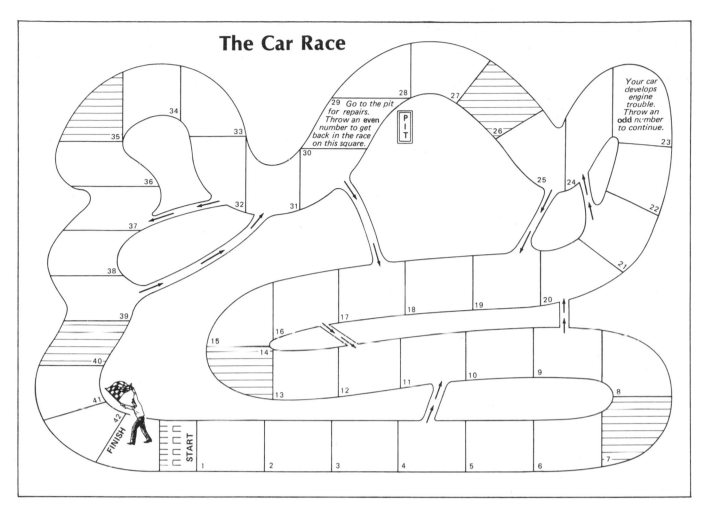

THE CAR RACE GAME

The striped squares are called 'Zebra Squares'. The 'zebra cards' (see below) contain penalty and bonus instructions. These cards are placed in front of the players.

Aim (There are two winners)

1   To be the first player to arrive on the square marked Finish. The teacher decides how many laps the players complete.

2   To be the player with the most points.

Rules

1   The player whose turn it is throws the dice and moves his counter the number of squares indicated by the dice. He reads the word on the square on which he has landed.

2   If a player lands on a square containing an arrow he follows the direction of the arrow and lands on another square; he reads the word on that square and on the square he has left.

3   If a player lands on a Zebra Square, he takes a zebra card and follows the instructions.

4   To win, a player must throw the exact number to reach the square marked Finish. If a player throws a higher number than he needs he does not move but reads the word on the square that corresponds to the number on the dice.

5   The points are totalled to see who has the most and is therefore the second winner.

If the teacher decides that play will continue for two or more laps it is advisable to make 'lap cards', e.g. four cards marked '1st lap' and four cards marked '2nd lap'. Each time a player passes the chequered flag he is awarded a lap card. It is then possible to ascertain who is 2nd, 3rd and 4th when the final lap has been completed.

Examples of zebra cards   (Draw lines on the back of these cards)

1   You get mud on your windscreen. Move back 4 squares.

2   You skid going round a corner. Move back 4 squares.

3   You are lying first in the race. Move forward 1 square.

4   Your car is running well. Have another turn.

NOTE: The teacher can use this game as a model and copy it on to a piece of card measuring approximately 795mm x 545mm. He should add four rectangles below the track. One is labelled 'lap cards', one, 'zebra cards' and the other two are labelled 'word cards'. The squares are left blank. The word cards from the chosen phonic unit are placed on one of the rectangles marked 'word cards', the lap cards and zebra cards are placed on the appropriate rectangles.

The rules are the same with the following exceptions: after the pupil has moved his counter the number of squares indicated by the dice, he picks up a word card, reads it and places it face upwards on the second rectangle marked 'word cards'.

To win, a player must throw the exact number to reach the Finish. He must read a word card for every throw which is higher than he needs.

THE POINTS OF THE COMPASS GAME

Preparation

1 On 18 cards write the following instructions:

(a) Move (1, 2, 3) squares up. (3 cards)

(b) Move (1, 2, 3) squares down. (3 cards)

(c) Move (1, 2, 3) squares to the right. (3 cards)

(d) Move (1, 2, 3) squares to the left. (3 cards)

(e) Move (1, 2, 3) squares diagonally to the right. (3 cards)

(f) Move (1, 2, 3) squares diagonally to the left. (3 cards)

2 Duplicate the model on p. 8 and place the 'points of the compass cards' on the appropriate rectangles (see opposite). Place the 'instruction cards' on the rectangle marked 'instruction cards 1'.

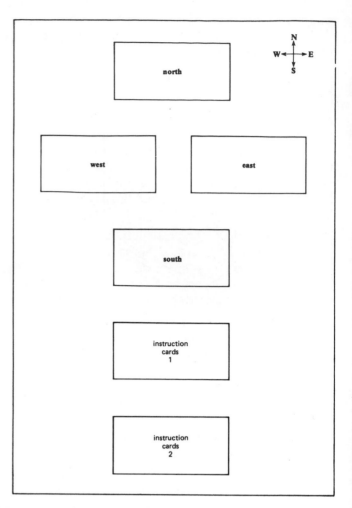

Points of the Compass

NORTH

43	44	45	46	47	48
42	41	40	39	38	37
31	32	33 *Have another turn*	34	35	36
30	29	28 *START HERE*	27	26	25
19 *Have another turn*	20	21	22	23	24
18	17	16	15	14	13 *Have another turn*
7	8	9	10	11	12
6	5	4	3	2	1

WEST · EAST

SOUTH

Aim

To be the player with the most points.

Rules

1 Pupils place their counters on square 28.

2 The player whose turn it is picks up an instruction card and moves his counter according to the instructions. He reads the word on the square on which he has landed and places the instruction card on the second rectangle marked 'instruction cards 2'.

3 If a player, following instructions, has to move his counter off the board, either North, South, East or West, he picks up the appropriate points of the compass card, e.g. if he leaves the upper part of the board marked North he takes a card marked North.

The points of the compass cards (see below) contain penalty and bonus points, and instructions which tell a player to return to a certain square on the board. The player reads the word on the square to which he has returned and gains a point if he reads it correctly.

4 When all the instruction cards have been used they are shuffled and replaced on the rectangle marked 'instruction cards 1'.

5 The teacher decides when the game ends. The points are totalled and the winner is the player with the most points.

Examples of points of the compass cards

North 1 Move to no. 17 and have another turn.

2 You are rude to the caretaker. Lose a point and move to no. 29.

3 Move to no. 21. If you can give the meaning of that word, gain another point.

South 1 You refuse to help your brother with his homework. Lose a point and move to no. 28.

2 You write a good story for English. Move to no. 14 and have another turn.

3 You are late for your History lesson. Lose a point and move to no. 27.

East 1 You take your sister to school every morning. Move to no. 16 and have another turn.

2 You learn all your spellings. Move to no. 33 and gain a point.

3 You forget to do your homework. Move to no. 20 and lose a point.

West 1 You do not do your homework. Move to no. 10 and miss a turn.

2 You are late for school. Lose a point and move to no. 32.

3 Move to no. 15. If you can give the meaning of that word, gain another point.

THE FOREST TRAIL, MOUNTAINEERING, PLANET X AND TREE GAMES

For these large board games the teacher will need to copy the models on pp. 9-12 by drawing on a piece of card measuring approximately 800 mm x 550 mm.

General Rules

1   Each player throws the dice; the player who gets the highest number starts. The order of play is clockwise.

2   If a player throws a six he takes another turn.

3   If a player lands on a penalty or bonus square he follows the instructions and reads a word.

THE FOREST TRAIL GAME

Preparation

Place the word cards face downwards on one of the rectangles marked 'word cards'. Place the 'danger cards' on the rectangle marked 'danger cards'.

Aim

1   To be the first player to arrive on the circle marked Home.

2   If the game is played in the alternative way (see below) the second winner is the player with most points.

Rules

1   The player whose turn it is throws the dice; moves his counter the number of squares indicated by the dice; picks up a word card, reads it and places it face upwards on the second rectangle marked 'word cards'. (Alternatively, the players keep each card they read correctly. When the last card has been taken, each player counts his cards and the teacher notes the number. Each card counts for one point. The cards are shuffled and replaced on the rectangle marked 'word cards' and the game continues. When one of the players has reached Home and won the game, the points are totalled to see who has the most.)

2   If a player lands on a Danger Point he takes a danger card (see below), reads it, follows the instructions and returns it to the bottom of the pack.

3   Once a player has passed Danger Point 1 the following rule applies: if a player's counter is landed on by another player's counter, he has to return to the previous Danger Point, e.g. if the counter is between Danger Point 2 and 3 he has to return it to the Danger Point 2. The player *does not* pick up a danger card in this situation.

4(a)   To win, a player must throw the exact number to reach Home. He must read a word card for

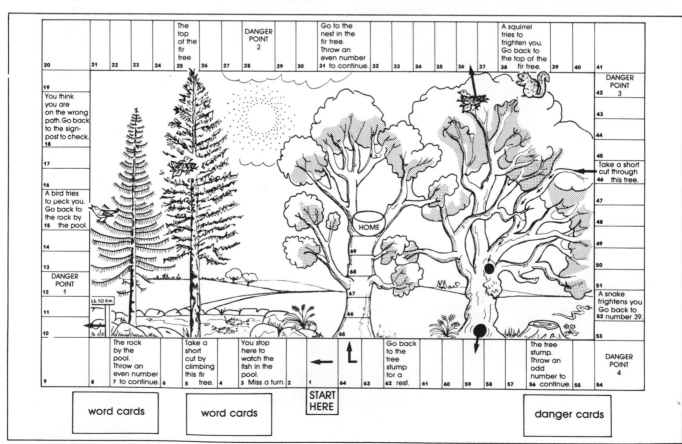

every throw which is higher than he needs.

(b) If the game is played in the alternative way, the points are totalled to see who has the most and is therefore the second winner.

Examples of danger cards

1 Go to the top of the fir tree. Throw an odd number to continue.

2 You sense danger. Go to no. 34.

3 It starts to rain, so you shelter under a tree. Miss a turn.

4 You see two huge dogs coming towards you. Have another turn to get clear of the danger.

5 If you haven't passed Danger Point 3 go to the nest in the fir tree. If you have passed Danger Point 3 go to the nest in the oak tree.

6 You are enjoying yourself and do not think you are in any danger. Have another turn.

THE MOUNTAINEERING GAME

Preparation

Place the word cards face downwards on one of the rectangles marked 'word cards'. Place the 'white

cloud cards' on the cloud marked 'white cloud cards' and the 'black cloud cards' on the cloud marked 'black cloud cards'.

Aim

1 To be the first player to reach the square marked Finish.

2 If the game is played in the alternative way the second winner is the player with the most points.

Rules

1 The player whose turn it is throws the dice; moves his counter the number of squares indicated by the dice; picks up a word card, reads it and places it face upwards on the second rectangle marked 'word cards' (for the alternative way to play this game see the instructions for the Forest Trail game, p. xvi).

2 If a player lands on a black or white cloud square, he takes a card (see below), follows the instructions and returns it to the bottom of the pack.

3(a) To win, a player must throw the exact number to reach the square marked Finish. He must read a word card for every throw which is higher than he needs.

(b) If the game is played in the alternative way, the points are totalled to see who has the most and is therefore the winner.

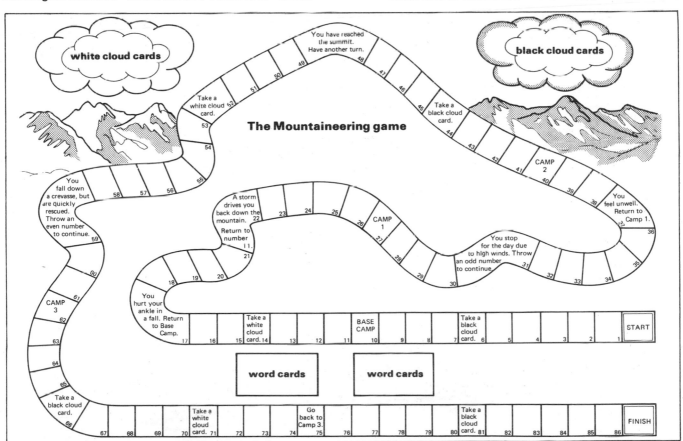

The Mountaineering game

Examples of black cloud cards

1 You fall and bruise your knee. Move back 4 squares.

2 You get left behind with the second party of climbers. Miss a turn.

3 You do not help your friend who has been injured. Move back 3 squares.

4 You feel ill and have a rest. Miss a turn.

Examples of white cloud cards

1 You are chosen to be one of the first climbers to reach the summit. Move forward 6 squares.

2 You stop for the night. It is very cold but you put your tent up quickly. Have another turn.

3 Your sherpas are very helpful. Move forward 5 squares.

4 The weather is fine and you make good progress. Have another turn.

THE PLANET X GAME

Preparation

Place the word cards face downwards on the rectangle marked 'word cards 1'. Place the 'orbit cards' on the rectangle marked 'orbit cards'.

Aim

1 To be the first player to arrive back at the Landing Pad on the part marked Finish Here.

2 If the game is played in the alternative way the second winner is the player with the most points.

Rules

1 Players orbit the planet first. The player whose turn it is throws the dice; moves his counter the number of squares indicated by the dice; picks up a word card, reads it and places it face upwards on the second rectangle marked 'word cards 2' (for the alternative way to play this game see the instructions for the Forest Trail game, p. xvi).

2 If a player lands on an orbit card square, he takes an orbit card (see below), follows the instructions and returns it to the bottom of the pack.

3 When a player has orbited the planet he lands on the planet. For example, if a player throws a five when his counter is on no. 36 he counts to no. 38 in the orbit circle, lands on the landing pad of the planet which is no. 39, and completes his throw of five by moving his counter another two places, stopping on no. 41.

4 To win, a player must throw the exact number to reach the part of the landing pad marked Finish Here. He must read a word card for every throw which is higher then he needs.

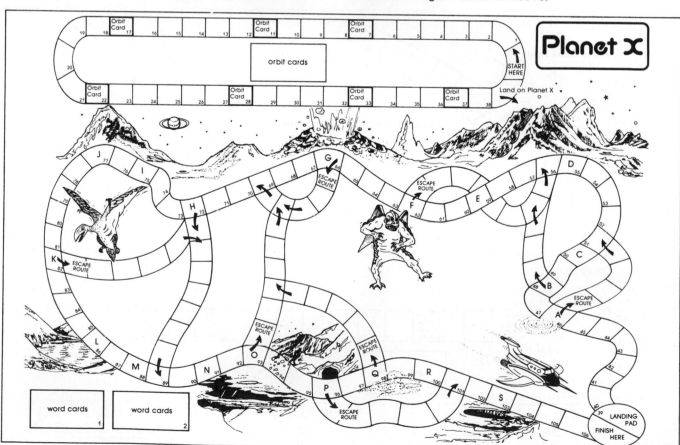

Examples of orbit cards

1   You have engine failure. Miss a turn.

2   You are in a meteorite storm. Go back 4 squares.

3   The controls of your spaceship do not work. Miss a turn while you mend them.

4   Another spaceship fires on you. Hurry forward three squares.

5   Your spaceship is moving slowly. Have another turn.

6   You are about to land on Planet X. Have another turn.

Key for the Planet X Game
(Write these instructions on the appropriate squares)

A   You nearly fall into a pool of quicksand and have to find an escape route.

B   You take a short cut.

C   You are a long way behind the others. Hurry on 5 squares.

D   You find some interesting rocks. Miss a turn to give yourself time to study them.

E   You decide to hurry. Go to the top of the mountain.

F   You have to escape from a fierce animal which blocks your way.

G   A volcano erupts and you have to escape from the streams of lava.

H   You find a secret tunnel and follow it.

I   You stop to watch another planet. Throw an odd number to continue.

J   **The top of the mountain.** Have another turn.

K   You have to escape from a huge bird which tries to kill you.

L   **The blue lake.** Rest here and miss a turn.

M   You have left your camera on the top of the mountain. Go back there to find it.

N   You fall into a deep hole. Miss a turn.

O   You have to find another route as your way is blocked by a fall of rocks.

P   It gets cold so you shelter in a cave. You have to escape when fierce men chase you out.

Q   You have to escape from a dust storm.

R   You have left your rock samples by the blue lake. Go back there to find them.

S   Your friend falls into a crater and you stop to rescue him. Miss a turn.

NOTE: It is a good idea to colour the Escape Routes to distinguish them from the numbered route.

THE TREE GAME

Preparation

Place the word cards face downwards on one of the rectangles marked 'word cards'. Place the 'risk cards' on the rectangle marked 'risk cards'.

Aim

To be the player with the most points.

Rules

1   The player whose turn it is throws the dice and moves his counter the number of squares indicated by the dice. Every time a player moves his counter his aim is to work out a route so that he lands on the square containing the most nuts.

2   When a player lands on a square containing nuts he takes the number of word cards indicated by the number of nuts. If he can read them he keeps them. Those he cannot read he returns to the bottom of the pack.

3   When the last card has been taken, each player counts his cards and the teacher notes the number each player has. Each card counts for one point. The cards are shuffled, replaced on the rectangle marked 'word cards' and the game continues.

4 If a player chooses to he may land on a Risk square. He takes a risk card (see below), follows the instructions and replaces the card at the bottom of the pack.

5 The players can move the counter in the following directions during one move:

either: upwards and to the left and right

or: downwards and to the left and right

The players must not move the counter both upwards and downwards during one move, or diagonally in any direction.

6 When a player reaches a square at the top of any branch he may move his counter to a square at the *top* of any other branch. He takes the number of cards indicated by the number of acorns on the square he has landed on.

7 The teacher decides when the game ends. The players count their cards and the teacher totals the number of points for each player. The winner is the player with the most points.

Examples of risk cards
(there are more bonus than penalty cards)

1 Gain one point.

2 Go to the birds' nest and have another turn.

3 Jump to any square you chose.

4 Go to the log and miss a turn.

5 Go to the top square of any branch.

6 Throw an odd number to continue.

7 Take 3 word cards.

Supplementary reading material

There is now a wide range of reading material specially designed for those pupils who are not yet ready for full-length novels but who require books with an adult approach, lively illustrations and a good story line.

In the series listed below the vocabulary is carefully graded to meet the needs of pupils with reading ages between 6.5 and 12+ years.

The following suggestions do not encompass the entire range but represent those series which have proved popular with senior pupils in one North London comprehensive school.

The teacher who is building up a library may find it useful to start with those series marked *. However, as some of these series contain over 20 titles it is advisable to obtain inspection copies first.

Edward Arnold

1 *Headlines.* 16 titles, e.g. *Survivors of the Sea, Remarkable Animals.* Reading Age 8 — 10.
2 *Action plays.* 5 titles, e.g. *Join the Action* (6 plays). *Action Replay* (7 plays). Ungraded.
3 *Databank, Remedial information books.* 12 titles, e.g. *Castles, Roads, Newspapers.*

Benn

1 Jimmy books. 3 titles, e.g. *Jimmy and the Ladder, Jimmy and the Plant Food.* RA 7 — 8.
2 *Inner Ring Hipsters. Red Circles.* 8 titles, e.g. *Sausages on the Shore, Digging for Treasure.* RA 7.5 — 8.

Black

Strands. * 10 titles, e.g. *Rebecca is a Cypriot; Shimon, Leah and Benjamin.* Aims to encourage an understanding of people from different cultural backgrounds.

Cape

Jets. 11 titles, e.g. *Sam Best Reporter* (short stories), *The Four Aces.* RA 8 — 9.

Cassell

1 *Red Lion.* 20 titles, e.g. *The Hanging Man, The Stolen Honda.* RA 8 — 9.
2 *Anchor.* 8 titles, e.g. *Attack in Dark Lane, Strangers in the Villages.* RA 8 — 10.

3 *Banjo.* 4 sets. 4 titles in each set, e.g. Set 1, *A Match on the Patch,* Set 2, *Dead on Time,* Set 3, *Down Rope Walk,* Set 4, *Smugglers' Haunt.* RA 7 — 8.
4 *Patchwork*
Level 1, 5 titles, e.g. *The Fallen Spaceman.* RA 8 — 9.
Level 2, 3 titles, e.g. *Surfboard.* RA 9 — 11.
Level 3, 3 titles, e.g. *Fight for Life.* RA 11+.
5 *Onward.* 8 titles, e.g. *Blackmailers' Hideout, Bomb in a Submarine.* RA 8 — 9.
6 *Solo.* 8 sets, 4 titles in each set, e.g. Set 5, *No Roads for the Wind, Lost.* RA 8 — 10.
7 *Disco.* 2 sets. 4 titles in each set, e.g. *Big Fish, Day off.*
8 *Discovery.* * 28 non-fiction topics divided into 7 sets, e.g. *Hobbies, Magic and Mystery, People.* RA 8 — 9.

Collins

1 *Collins English Library.* 6 levels (4 suitable for the Remedial Department).
Level 1, 7 titles, e.g. *Inspector Holt and the Fur Van.* RA 7+.
Level 2, 9 titles, e.g. *The Canterville Ghost.* RA 8+.
Level 3, 8 titles, e.g. *Gunshot Grand Prix.* RA 9+.
Level 4, 7 titles, e.g. *King Solomon's Mines.* RA 10+.
2 *Trigger,* 6 titles, e.g. *Hot Foot Nat, Out West.* RA 8 — 9.

Dent

1 *The Manxman.* 6 titles, e.g. *The Old Bike, The Speedway.* RA 6 — 7.
2 *The Raft on the River.* 6 titles, e.g. *Happy Meeting, A Big Fish.* RA 7 — 8.

Evans

Checkers. 3 themes, 4 titles in each, e.g. *Family, Lost and Found, Sport, Footballs for Schoolkids, Authority, Fair Game.* RA 8 — 10.

Gibson

The Look-out Gang. 6 titles, e.g. *The Gang Meets, The Gang and the Pay Grab.* RA 6 — 8.

Ginn

1 *Approach Trend.* 9 titles, e.g. *Last Train, Red Surf.* RA 6.5 — 7.

2 *Mainstream Trend.* 42 titles, e.g. *The Dark House, Danger Ride.* RA 7.5 — 8.5.

3 *Trendset.* 16 titles, e.g. *Coffee at Charlies, Cry on a Foggy Night.* RA 9 — 10.

Harrap

Reporters. 16 titles, e.g. *Top Sport, Top Soccer.* RA 8 — 10.

Hart-Davis

1 *Adventures in Space.* 12 titles.
Series 1, *Moonflight books* 1 — 3, *Journey to Mars* 1 — 3.
Series 2, *Red Planet* 1 — 3, *Journey to a New Earth* 1 — 3.

2 *Scanners.* This series presents the basic facts about important issues, e.g. drugs, alcohol, crime.

3 *Solos.* Stages 1 — 6 *Only a Dream* (Stage 1) *Tea Break* (Stage 6). RA 6 — 8.5.

Heinemann

1 *Stories for Today.* First series, 6 titles, e.g. *Ron's Fight, Ginger and Sharon.* RA 9 and below. Second series, 6 titles e.g. *June's Work. Rescue at Night.* RA 9 — 10.

2 *Heinemann's Guided Readers.* Beginner level, 14 titles, e.g. *Rich Man, Poor Man, Marco.* RA 8.

3 *Instant Reading.* 8 titles, e.g. *The Iron Man, The Conquest of Mars.* RA 9.

Hulton

1 *Inswingers.* Football theme with 6 titles, e.g. *Les Joins United, Les's First Match.* RA 8 — 10.

2 *Speedwingers.* Motor-cycle racing theme with 6 titles, e.g. *A Scramble for Steve, Steve Takes a Chance.* RA 8 — 10.

3 *Popswingers.* Pop group theme with 6 titles, e.g. *Rock on Speech Day, First Gig.* RA 8 — 10.

Hutchinson

1 *Spirals.** 20 titles, e.g. *The Ear, Dreams.* RA 7 — 8.

2 *Spirals* (plays). * 4 titles, 3 plays in each book, *An Earwig in the Ear, The Good, the Bad and the Bungle.*

3 *Bulls-Eye,* 35 titles, e.g. *Jaws, Dr No.* RA 9 — 10.

4 *Falcon Comics.** 4 titles, e.g. *Tram Fury, The Rocket Rumble.* RA 7 — 8.

Ladybird

Robin Hood. 4 titles, e.g. *The Silver Arrow, Robin Hood Outlawed.* RA 7 — 10.

LDA (Learning Development Aids)

Picture Phonic Crossword Cards.

Longman

1 *Squirrels.** Stages 1 — 5. 26 titles, e.g. *The Prince and the Pauper* (Stage 2), *The Adventures of Sherlock Holmes* (Stage 4). Stage 1, vocabulary 450 words; Stage 5, vocabulary 1800 words.

2 *Structural Readers.* Stages 1 — 6, e.g. *Car Thieves* (Stage 1), *The Last Experiment* (Stage 3).

3 *Structural Readers* (plays). 4 titles, e.g. *Three Mystery Plays, Mystery on the Moor.*

4 *Books in Easy English.* (Stages 1 and 2 only*) Stages 1 — 4, e.g. *Telling my Fortune* (Stage 1), *UFOs* (Stage 2). Both books contain short stories.

5 *Bangers and Mash.* 14 titles, e.g. *The Hat Trick, Eggs.* RA 6 — 8. (Upper junior interest age.)

Macdonald

1 *Ghosts.* 6 titles, e.g. *Caesar's Ghost, Macbeth the Murderer King.* RA about 8.

2 *Adventures.* 11 titles, e.g. *Curse of the Pharaohs, The Battle of the Alamo.* RA 8.

3 *Mysteries.* 6 titles, e.g. *The Marie-Celeste, Atlantis.* RA 8.

4 *Focus on Sport.* 6 titles, e.g. *Motor-racing, Athletics.* RA about 7.5.

5 *Action World.* 6 titles, e.g. *Sport, The Space Age.* RA between 6.5 and 8.5.

Macmillan

1 *Crown Street Kings.* 18 titles, e.g. *Meet Harry King. The Milk Round.* RA 8.

2 *Club 75.* 17 titles, e.g. *The Goalkeeper's Revenge, All for the Rovers.* RA 8 — 10.

3 *Flag.* 40 titles, e.g. *Copper Cove, Finders Keepers.* RA 8 — 10.

Methuen

1 *Jim Hunter**
Level 1, 2 titles, e.g. *Jim and the Sun Goddess.* RA 7 — 8.
Level 2, 10 titles, e.g. *The Desert Chase.* RA 8 — 9.

2 *Terraced House Books.* 4 sets, e.g. *The Launderette, The Supermarket* (Set B). Multi-ethnic, everyday activities and interests. (For beginners.)

John Murray

1 *Bestellers.* 30 titles, e.g. *Flight to Fear, Black Beach.* RA 8 — 9.

2 *Galaxy 5.* 6 titles, e.g. *On the Red World, Dead Moon.* RA 8 — 9.

3 *Laura Brewster.* 6 titles, e.g. *House of Laughs, Tiger Rose.* RA 8 — 9.

4 *The Tufton Hill Lot.* 6 plays featuring a group of boys and girls in an inner city setting. RA 8 — 10.

Nelson

*Help.** 3 sets. RA 6 — 8.

1 *First Helping.* 6 titles, e.g. *The Spy, Ghosts.*

2 *Help Story Books.* 6 titles, e.g. *The Night I felt a Ghost, The Day We Found Fang Island.*

3 *Help Yourself.* 6 titles, e.g. *The Man in the Black Jacket, Witches' Wood.*

Oxford University Press

1 *English Picture Readers. The World's Great Stories.** 13 titles, e.g. *Hercules, Robin Hood.* RA 7 — 9.

2 *Pictorial Classics.** 8 titles, e.g. *Treasure Island, Robinson Crusoe,* RA 9 — 10.

3 *Oxford Progressive English Readers.* Grade 1, 17 titles, e.g. *Oliver Twist.* 1900 Headwords. Grade 2, 13 titles, e.g. *A Tale of Two Cities.* 2900 Headwords. Grade 3, 23 titles, e.g. *From Russia With Love.* 3500 Headwords.

The following books are also useful:

Bartholomews: *Our World Atlas.*

Black: *Black's Writing Dictionary.**

Evans: *The Zebra Dictionary in Colour.*

Harrap: *English Sign Language.*

Macmillan: *Our World Encyclopedia.*

Nisbet: *A First Dictionary.*

Suppliers of materials

Philip & Tacey Ltd, North Way, Andover, Hampshire, SP10 5BA.

In addition to the materials listed below, Philip & Tacey stock a full range of teaching aids, stationery and equipment and will send their comprehensive catalogues on request.

1   Garland mounting boards for mounting the duplicated games (assorted colours). Size 321mm x 266mm. Catalogue no. 023-082-080.

2   Carnival coloured card (assorted colours). Size 533mm x 475mm. Catalogue no. 023-083-010.

3   Plastic wallets, useful for storing the danger, risk, cloud, and points of the compass cards. Size 195mm x 135mm. Catalogue no. 5264 (265-8).

4   Counters (5 colours). Catalogue no. N477-1.

Don Greswell Ltd, Bridge House, Grange Park, London N21 1RB.

Book cards for the listed words in each phonic unit and for bonus and penalty cards in the games (green, pink, blue, white, buff). Standard size.

For GLC and ILEA Schools: both authorities supply the following materials (stock numbers from the GLC/ILEA Catalogue).

1   Transparent plastic self-adhesive book covering. Size 70mm x 210mm, no. 100431. Size 20m x 500mm, no. 100418.

2   Box files no. 152483.

3   Folders, A4 (assorted colours), to hold the pupils' completed worksheets, e.g. Orange no. 205835.

4   Laces for the folders (box of 100). Size 152mm, no. 179328.

5   'Twinlock' crystal files complete with tabs and inserts (50). No. 307010. If the worksheets are duplicated in quantity they can be stored in a filing cabinet, using the 'Twinlock' suspended filing system.

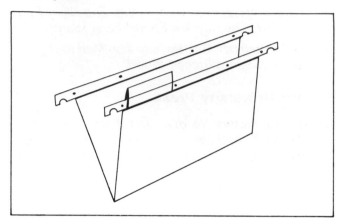

6   Card index box, useful for storing the Butterfly and Castle games. Size 200mm x 125mm x 145mm deep. No. 160075.

7   Dice, 6-sided. No. (A)D 311377.

8   Book cards for the listed words in each phonic unit and for bonus and penalty cards in the games. Size 100mm x 50mm. Blue no. 180511. Yellow no. 180524. Price 19p per hundred (1981).

W.H. Smith, Ryman, or any large stationers stock all the above items except the book cards.

Large-sized card, 795mm x 545mm, for the four board games, can be obtained from most art shops.

Celsur Plastics Ltd, Norfolk House, Drake Avenue, Gresham Rd, Staines, Middx.

Pocket, with punch holes, for storing master sheets.

Some accepted tests

for assessing a pupil's ability

Screening and attainment

1 *Salford Sentence Reading Test.* Forms A, B and C. Age range 6.0 — 10.5. Individual test published by Hodder & Stoughton.

2 *Young's SPAR Test* (spelling and reading), Forms A and B. Age range 7.0 — 16.0. Group test published by Hodder & Stoughton.

Diagnostic tests

1 Non-verbal, to assess ability level (IQ)

(a) *NFER* Non-verbal BD. Age range 8.5 — 11.5. Group Test.

(b) *NFER* Non-verbal DH. Age range 10.0 — 15.0. Group test.

2 Phonic Skills

(a) *The Swansea Test of Phonic Skills:* for pupils whose reading age falls below 7.5. Individual and group test published by Basil Blackwell, Oxford.

(b) *The Assessment of Reading Ability:* The West Sussex Education Committee's Psychological Service staff members have produced this excellent booklet (50p in 1981). It contains all the tests needed to diagnose a pupil's strengths and weaknesses (phonic ability, visual and auditory discrimination). It also gives detailed information about a wide range of reading tests with a brief description and evaluation of each one. Copies of this booklet may be obtained from the Education Department, County Hall, Chichester, West Sussex.

(c) *The Domain Phonic Test Kit.* Age range 5.0 — 9.0. Individual test. Contains 4 individual diagnostic tests of phonic knowledge and 1 of auditory discrimination. Published by Oliver & Boyd.

3 Visual Perception Materials
The Look Tests. Published by Macmillan.

Reading Accuracy, Comprehension and Speed

The Neal Analysis of Reading Ability. Age range 6.0 — 12.0. (Supplementary diagnostic tests are in the test booklet.) Individual test published by Macmillan.

Reading Comprehension

The Wide-Span Reading Test. Age range 7.0 — 15.0. Group test published by Nelson.

Spelling

1 *Young's SPAR Test* (spelling and reading). Age range 7.0 — 16.0. Published by Hodder & Stoughton.

2 *Daniels and Diack Graded Spelling Test 11.*

A battery of diagnostic tests, including tests for visual and auditory discrimination, is included in the following:

1 *The Standard Reading Test* by Daniels and Diack (book) published by Chatto & Windus.

2 *The Aston Index* (boxed material) published by LDA (Learning Development Aids).

Notes on using the worksheets

The worksheets may be duplicated by teachers for use within the classroom.

Most of the worksheets are self-explanatory, but before worksheets marked * are used the relevant notes should be read.

All pupils need to be taught the signs of the long and short sounds of the vowels as these are used in some of the worksheets.

As most reading material for slow learners of secondary age is written in the past tense, pupils will meet the suffix **ed** in the first stories they read. The teacher can explain the three sounds of **ed** (see p. I2) and reinforce the rule when necessary.

The worksheets are arranged in sections which are listed alphabetically.

A2, A3 (The alphabet 1 and 2)

The alphabet is an aid for those teachers who are dealing with pupils whose reading age falls below 7.0 years. Although the reading age is only an approximate guide to each pupil's level of attainment it usually gives a good indication of ability. For pupils whose reading age falls below 7.5 years, the alphabet worksheets may also be used as a quick test for letter and sound, upper and lower case recognition.

A4 (The alphabet 3)

Pupils should learn the words 'vowel' and 'consonant'. They should also learn the signs which denote the long and short sounds of the vowels, as these are used in later worksheets: the short vowel sound is denoted by ˘ placed over the vowel, e.g. **săt**; the long vowel sound is denoted by ‾ placed over the vowel, e.g. **nāme**.

The teacher should emphasise that the long sound is the *name* of the vowel and the short sound is the *sound* of the vowel.

The short sound of the vowels is easily forgotten and needs constant revision. The teacher could encourage the pupils to remember the pictures on this page in order to recall the short sound of the vowels, e.g. to recall the short sound of a they visualise a cat.

The teacher can explain to pupils who are working systematically through sections A — E that the a in this and subsequent worksheets will be the normal **a** used in printed books.

A7 (The note in the bottle)

The teacher reads the introduction, or the pupils read the words they know with the teacher supply-

ing those words they have not yet learnt. (The note reads: 'Help! My boat sank. I am here.') At this level it is almost impossible to write material of high interest unless more difficult words are included. Therefore teachers will need to be prepared to give pupils the maximum amount of help. This applies to all the worksheets in sections A — E.

A9, A10 (Basic words 1 and 2)

Pupils must learn to read these words as sight words and learn how to spell them later. The teacher can play a variety of games using these words and this should help pupils to learn them fairly quickly. Make sure pupils understand the instruction, 'Choose from the words that are underlined.'

See also Crosswords below.

A11, A12 (Word endings 1 and 2 —these are final blends)

It may seem a big jump from 'Basic words' to 'Word endings'. However, many of the listed words, or words ending in these final blends, are included in books written for the older pupil with a reading age of 6.0 to 7.0 years. These final blends may be taught now but teachers can return to them later to reinforce the learning.

Word endings 1: The teacher can point out that all the vowels have a short sound except in the words **find** and **pint**.

Word endings 2: The teacher can point out that all the vowels have a short sound except in the words ending in **old**.

Crosswords

The crosswords could initially be introduced by pupils making up their own simple crosswords. To introduce the idea of words being linked horizontally and vertically pupils may use these or similar patterns.

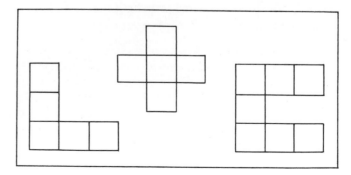

Pupils can make up clues orally or write a simple sentence containing the word. The phrases 'clues across' and 'clues down' can be taught here.

To familiarise pupils with the idea of numbering, the following method of instruction may be used with the first crossword. (This method is useful for any pupils who are attempting a crossword for the first time.)

(a) Put your finger on no. 1.
(b) Run your finger across the blank squares. This is called 1 across.
(c) Put your finger on no. 1 again.
(d) Run your finger down the blank squares. This is called 1 down.
(e) Find the clue for 1 across.
(f) Find the clue for 1 down.

Then the teacher can choose a numbered square at random and ask the pupils whether the clue is across or down. Use many examples. To reinforce understanding the teacher can draw a six- or eight-squared crossword on the board and work with the pupils in compiling it.

One useful aid is *Picture Phonic Crossword Cards* published by Learning Development Aids.

The crosswords in sections A — E may be completed as a group exercise. The teacher supplies any words the pupils have not yet learnt.

B1, B2, B3 (Short and long vowels)

A useful rule for short and long vowels is as follows: when two vowels come together or are separated by a single consonant, the first vowel usually says its own name, which is the long sound, and the second vowel is silent, e.g. pāin, sāme, rēad, sēen, bīte, tūbe. There are, however, many exceptions to this rule, some of which are given on pp. L10 and L12.

In a very short word containing one vowel, the vowel usually has a short sound. Some exceptions are: be, he, she, me, we, by, my, cry, etc.

The letters y and w function as vowels when they come at the end of a word or syllable, e.g. cry, myself (see vowel y, p. G4), low, showing.

It is not essential to make pupils learn the phonic rules. Some pupils find them too difficult to learn and prefer to make up their own strategies for learning vocabulary. The phonic approach should in any case be only one element in the teaching of reading. However, there are some pupils who seem able both to learn the phonic rules and to enjoy applying them.

B4 (ai and ay)

The teacher can point out that the pronunciation of say changes when an s is added.

B6 (ea)

The teacher can point out that the ear in tear can also be pronounced like the air in chair and this changes the meaning of the word; the ear in bear and pear has the same sound.

B8 (ea, ee; The message)

As the pupils do not know the content of the message they will not use capital letters for the proper names. After the pupils have completed this exercise the teacher may like to teach them some of the rules regarding the use of capital letters.

The message reads:

Pete,
    We shall meet next week in the Mean Man Café for a meal. You will see the keys of the jeep on one of the seats. Keep to the sea road then turn left at Leaf Lane. This lane leads to the cafe .
There is no need to fear Ben. He is weak and I will deal with him.
                    Team Leader

In part B point out that each pair of words sea, see, meet, meat, has the same sound but a different spelling and meaning. The teacher can return to the ea and ee worksheets on the previous two pages and show pupils the following homophones: week, weak, heel, heal, reel, real, been, bean, seem, seam.

C1 (Silent e; i+e)

Make sure that pupils know the meaning of 'etc.'. Point out that the i in give and live has a short sound.

D1 (r blends)

(Some teachers may prefer to teach the sh and ch rules before the blends.)

All the r blends are grouped together as the rule is fairly easy to apply. However, the teacher may feel that pupils who work at a much slower pace can only assimilate one or two of the seven blends during one lesson. As the exercise contains words from all seven lists of blends, these pupils can complete the exercise after two or three lessons. (This applies to l, s and three-letter blends.)

It is important to make sure that pupils understand what is meant by true and false. Point out that the **y** in the words **cry**, **dry**, **fry** and **try** is a vowel and has the sound of a long **i**.

The concept of opposites may be introduced when completing question 2 of this exercise.

NOTE: The blends can be further reinforced by playing the Car Race game (see p. xiii) in the following way: instead of writing words on each square of the playing board, write one **r** blend (this can be done with **l** and **s** blends on other boards) on each square and repeat at random until every square contains a blend. (Each pupil has his own board.) The pupil says the blend on the square on which he has landed then picks up a word card from the pile with the appropriate blend written beneath it and reads the word (see below).

On a large piece of card measuring approximately 500mm x 300mm draw 7 rectangles and write a blend below each one, e.g.

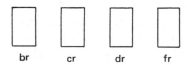

Write all the words from the **r** blend worksheet on word cards and place them on the appropriate rectangles.

It is a good idea to distinguish between the seven different blends by writing each set of words in different colours. This facilitates sorting which can be done by the pupils.

D3 (**s** blends)

The **st** blends are the most often used and may need reinforcing with additional material.

E1 (**sh**)

The teacher can point out that the **u** in push (column 3) has the sound of **oo** as in **book**. Make sure that pupils understand the instruction, 'Choose from the words that are underlined.'

E4 (**tch**)

The teacher can point out that all the vowels have a short sound except for the **a** in **watch** (column 2) and the **u** in **butcher** (column 6).

E5, E6, E7 (**ch** saying **k** and **ch** saying **sh**)

These rules can be taught at a later stage. However, after teaching the sound of **ch** on p. E2 the teacher can explain that familiar words such as stomach, ache, anchor and Christmas do not follow this rule.

E8 (**th**)

Although it is not necessary for pupils to learn the difference between a voiced and a voiceless **th**, it is essential to show them the difference in the tongue's position when pronouncing **th**, as many children pronounce **th** as **f**.

E9 (**wh**)

Before pupils say the words in column 4 the teacher can point out that the **o** in **who**, **whose** and **whom** is pronounced like the **oo** in **moon** and the **w** is silent.

The cities which are mentioned in questions 1, 3 and 5 are difficult to pronounce and the teacher will probably have to show pupils their position on the map.

It is also useful to have ready a picture of The Needles so that pupils can complete question 4. Before starting question 5a the meaning of 'capital city' may need to be explained and the teacher can ask pupils to find other capital cities on the relevant map in the atlas.

E11 (**ck**)

Make sure that pupils understand the instruction, 'Change the first letter of the old word to make a new word that fits the new meaning', as it is repeated in later worksheets. Practise with the following pairs of words before completing this or a similar exercise: rang, sang, sing, king, sink, pink, felt, belt. The pupils can supply the meaning of the second word. Pupils need to learn the concept of rhyming at this stage.

The worksheets in the first five sections, A — E, should be followed systematically with slow-learning pupils of a low reading age (6.0 — 7.0 years). These rules should be grasped thoroughly before pupils proceed to the next sections.

The work in sections F — S should be taught according to the needs of the group (see section on assessment). The rules increase in difficulty throughout this section *but it is not intended that all pupils should work systematically through every rule.*

F1 — F5 (Three letter blends)

For pupils who have systematically followed the rules in sections A — E, these rules may be taught at a later stage. The teacher can introduce pupils to the three-letter blends by playing pelmanism (or any other game) with the following familiar words: strange, street, strong, strength, straight, scream, splash, three, throw, through.

G3 (Syllables)

Explain that each syllable must contain one or more vowels and that usually the number of vowel sounds equals the number of syllables. However, in final syllables like **ble, cle, dle, fle, gle, ple, tle**, the **e** is silent and sometimes only the **l** is sounded. The teacher can show pupils how to divide words into syllables, e.g. ar/row, vi/o/lin.

G6 (Colours)

The pattern can be coloured symmetrically. The concept of a symmetrical pattern may need to be explained.

H1 (ain)

Exceptions to this rule are as follows: the **ain** in **mountain** and **captain** is pronounced as **in**; the **ain** in **Britain**, **curtain** and **certain** is pronounced as **tn**. (These words appear in later worksheets.)

H3 (ight)

When teaching the sound **ight** point out that the following words have the same sound: bite, kite, site, white, polite. In the word **height** attention should be called to the silent **e**.

Section I

For slow-learning pupils who are working systematically through the scheme this section may be taught at a later stage. Teachers can explain the suffixes and contractions when they occur in the stories or worksheets pupils are reading.

I1 (The suffix ing)

Make sure pupils know the meaning of 'root word'. In part C make sure pupils know the meaning of the phrase 'double the last letter'. (This rule applies to words which end in a single vowel and a consonant.)

I2, I3 (The suffix ed)

These worksheets can be used for revision and reinforcement of the suffix **ed** and, as pupils use most of these words in their written work, they should learn the spellings.

I6 (Contractions 1)

The teacher can point out the missing letters in the first word of the contractions **can't, shan't** and **won't**; also that **cannot** is one word.

J4 (er)

The teacher can point out the soft **g** in **danger** and **passenger**.

Word search solution:

t					r			s	h	i	v	e	r
e				e	e								
m			d		m			d	a	n	g	e	r
p		n			e				b				r
e	u		n	u	m	b	e	r			u		e
r					b						t		
	p				e					t	w	t	
		a			r	n			e		a	e	
			p				t	l			t		r
				e			e				e		
s	u	m	m	e	r	r		r			r		

A few examples of exceptions to this rule are as follows:

er: serial, hero, experiment.
ir: fire, hire, wire, admire, retire, direct, pirate, giraffe.
ur: sure, insure, bury, during, jury.

J8 (ture)

For slow-learning pupils who are working systematically through the scheme this rule may be taught at a later stage. The teacher can introduce pupils to the words **picture, adventure, puncture** and **mixture** as these words are used more often.

K1 (ar)

Note: When **ar** is immediately preceded by **w**, it usually has the sound of **or** as in **for**. Examples: war, warm, warn, ward, reward, towards, wardrobe, swarm.

K2 (ar followed by e)

The teacher can explain that although there is a **c** between the **r** and **e** in **scarce** (column 5), the **ar** is still pronounced as **air**.

K5 (or)

NOTE: When **or** is immediately preceded by **w** it usually has the sound of **er** in **her**. Examples: word, work, world, worm, worse, worth.

When **or** is at the end of a word of more than one syllable, it usually has the sound of **er** in **butter**. Examples: doctor, conductor, actor, inspector.

L8 (ou as in cloud)

Point out that the b in doubt (column 3) is silent. In part A the teacher may need to explain the meaning of 'past tense'. In part B pupils may need an atlas.

M1 (The soft sound of g; g before e)

Pupils will need an atlas for this lesson.

M2 (The soft sound of g; g before i and y)

Some exceptions to this rule are: give, girl, giggle, gift, begin.

M3 (age)

The teacher can point out that garage (column 1) can also be pronounced like mirage. It may be necessary to explain how to obtain the average of a set of numbers in question 4.

M5 (dge)

The teacher can point out that when e is followed by t the e is pronounced as a short i. When e is followed by r the er is pronounced like the er in butter.

N2 (The soft sound of c; difficult words)

The teacher can omit this worksheet from the sequence of the soft sound of g and c if he feels it will be too difficult at this point. If it is omitted and taught at a later stage, he must teach the words receipt, certainly, centre and cell before pupils attempt the 'c before e crossword'.

N4 (The soft sound of c; c before i)

The teacher can point out that in recipe (column 4) the final e is sounded. The final e is also sounded in the words apostrophe and catastrophe.

N5 (The soft sound of c; c before y)

Pupils will need an atlas for this worksheet.

O3 (More silent letters)

The teacher can read each word and ask the pupils to say which letter (consonant, not vowel) is silent.

P1 (au)

The following words can be taught as exceptions to the general rule: au as a short o: Australia, Austria, because, cauliflower, sausage, fault; au as ar: aunt, laugh.

The message reads: 'The audience is exhausted.'

P4, P5 (qu 1 and 2)

The teacher can point out that the a in the first five words in column 2 should be pronounced as a short o.

The password is 'question quietly'.

In part B the teacher can tell pupils that they may add a suffix to the words.

P6 (squ)

The teacher can point out that the a in the first five words in columns 1 and 2 should be pronounced as a short o.

Q5 (sion)

Sion says zh'n when it comes after a vowel. It says sh'n when it comes after a consonant. It is difficult to explain the zh'n symbol and pupils tend to remember sion as sh'n.

In question 6, the teacher can point out that the initials M.I. stand for Military Intelligence and the number indicates the department.

R1 (ought–ort, ough–ō)

The teacher may need to supply the meaning and pronunciation of thoroughly (in the story). He can point out that borough has a similar pronunciation to thorough.

R4 (ou–ŭ, ough–ŭff)

The letter reads:

Dear Mum and Dad,
   The going is *rough* but we are not having any *trouble* passing through the *country* villages. There is *enough* food as we now have *double* rations. *Courage* is our motto and the men are *tough* and *young* enough to overcome the hardships.
   The captain's *cousin* trod on a land mine yesterday. You only have to *touch* these mines to be blown to pieces. Poor man!
   We are now only a *couple* of miles from Paris which we will enter tomorrow or the next day. I hope this terrible war will soon be over.
                    Love,
                    Tony

S1 (cial, cious – ci says sh)

The teacher can point out that the ti in the words initial and confidential is also pronounced as sh. In part B, the teacher may need to explain the meaning of the word 'adjective'.

Index to worksheets

Story sheet

Name .... Form ....

Title of story ....

....

....

....

....

....

....

....

....

Spelling box .... *Name* .... *Form* ....

1	5	9 ....
2	6	10 ....
3	7	11 ....
4	8	12 ....

Play sheet

Name .... Form ....

Title of play ....

Characters ....

....

....

....

....

....

Scene ....

....

....

....

....

....

....

....

....

....

....

....

....

....

....

Spelling box	Name	Form ....
1	5	9 ....
2	6	10 ....
3	7	11 ....
4	8	12 ....

Checklist *Form* ....

Date:						
Names	RA	RA	RA	SA	SA	SA

A	alphabet : names	
	sounds	
	short vowels	
	basic words 1 & 2	
	final blends 1 & 2	

B	long vowels : a + e	
	ai, ay	
	ea	
	ee	

C	i + e	
	o + e	
	oa	
	u + e	

D	blends : r	
	l	
	s	

E	diagraphs : sh	
	ch	
	tch	
	ch saying k	
	ch saying sh	
	th	
	wh	
	ck	

F	3-letter blends : str	
	scr, spr, spl	
	thr, shr	

G	a saying ŭ	
	compound words	
	syllables	
	vowel y	
	days of week, months	
	colours	

H	ain	
	all, alk	
	ight	

I	suffixes : ing	
	ed	
	ly	
	contractions	

J	o͞o, o͝o	
	er, ir, ur	
	ew	
	ture	
	ble, cle, dle	
	fle, gle, ple, tle	

K	ar	
	ar + e	
	or	
	aw	

L	oi	
	oy	
	ow (long ō)	
	ow as in cow	
	ou as in cloud	
	different sounds of ea, ei	
	different sounds of ie, ui, ua, ue	

M	soft g : g before e	
	g before i & y	
	age	
	dge	

N	soft c : c before e	
	c before i	
	c before y	

O	silent letters : kn, gn	
	wr, mb	
	more silent letters	

P	au	
	qu	
	squ	

Q	tion	
	sion	
	ph	

R	ought (ort), ough (ŏ)	
	our (-er)	
	ou (o͞o, o͝o)	
	ou (ŭ), ough (ŭff)	
	ous, ious	

S	cial, cious	
	cian	

Books read

The Butterfly game

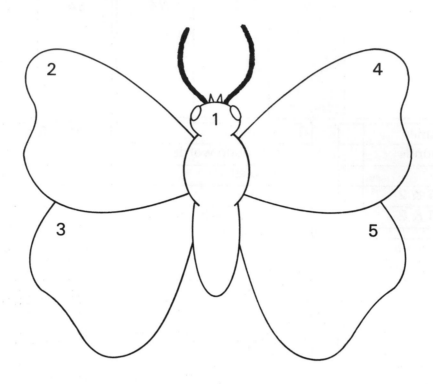

The Castle game

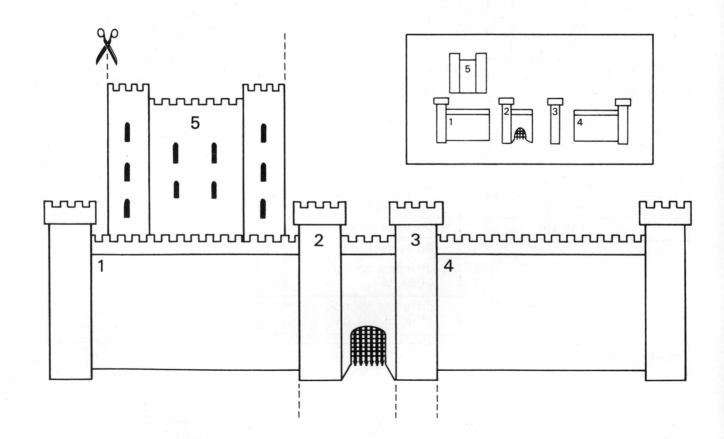

Secret Passages

41

42

43

44 *Throw an odd number to continue*

45

46

47

HALL
START and FINISH HERE

40

31

30

21

20 *Go to the loft*

11

10

1

39

32

29

22

19

12

9

2

38

33

28

23

18

13 *Go to the cellar*

8 *Go to the cellar*

3

37

34 *Go to the loft*

27

24 *Go to the cellar*

17

14

7

4

36

35

26

25

16

15

6

5 *Have another turn*

LOFT

For your next turn: multiply the number you get by 6. The total is the number of the square you move to.

CELLAR

For your next turn: multiply the number you get by 2. The total is the number of the square you move to.

The Car Race

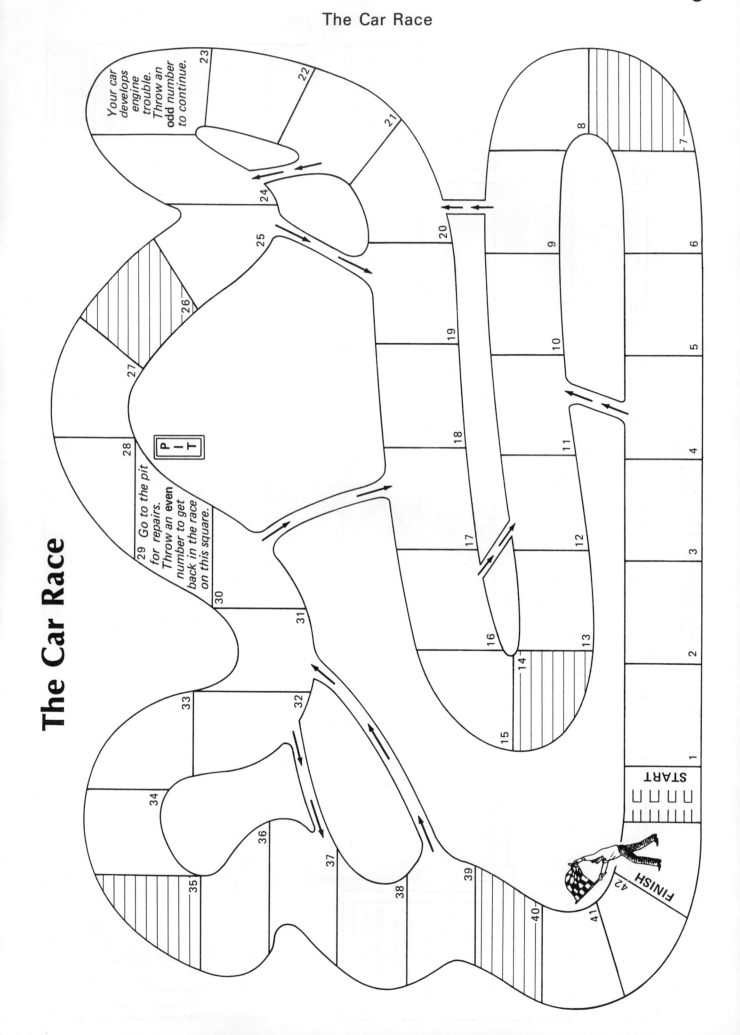

23

22

21

24

Your car develops engine trouble. Throw an odd number to continue.

25

8

7

20

9

6

26

19

10

5

27

18

11

4

P - I - T

28

17

12

3

29 Go to the pit for repairs. Throw an even number to get back in the race on this square.

16

13

2

30

31

15

1

START

32

33

14

34

36

37

38

39

FINISH

35

40

41

42

Points of the Compass

Points of the Compass

NORTH

EAST

WEST

SOUTH

43	44	45	46	47	48
42	41	40	39	38	37
31	32	33	34	35	36
30	29	28 (*START HERE*)	27	26	25
19	20	21	22	23	24
18	17	16	15	14	13
7	8	9	10	11	12
6	5	4	3	2	1

Have another turn (square 34)

Have another turn (square 24)

Have another turn (square 30)

Points of the Compass

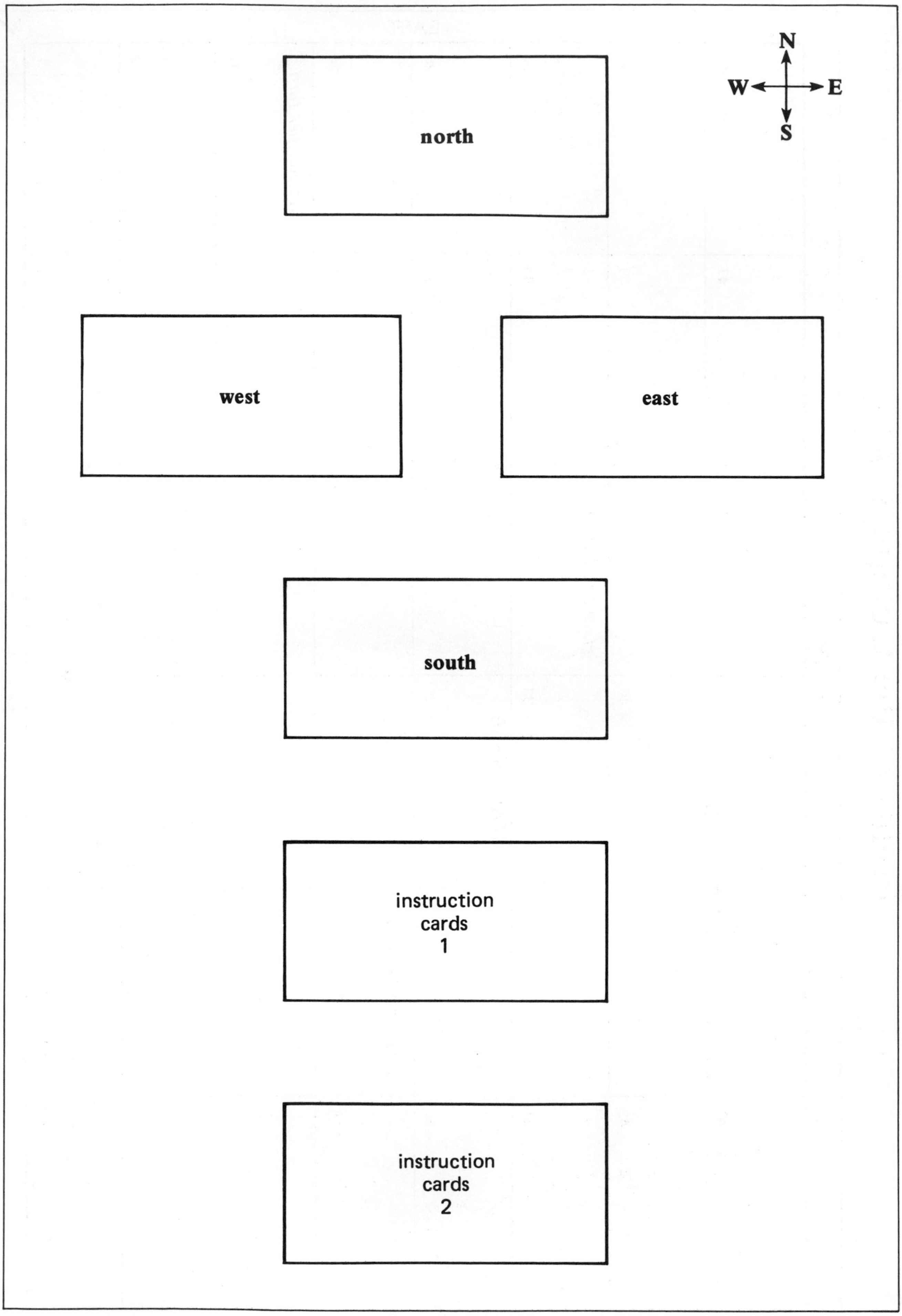

N

W ← → E

S

north

west

east

south

instruction
cards
1

instruction
cards
2

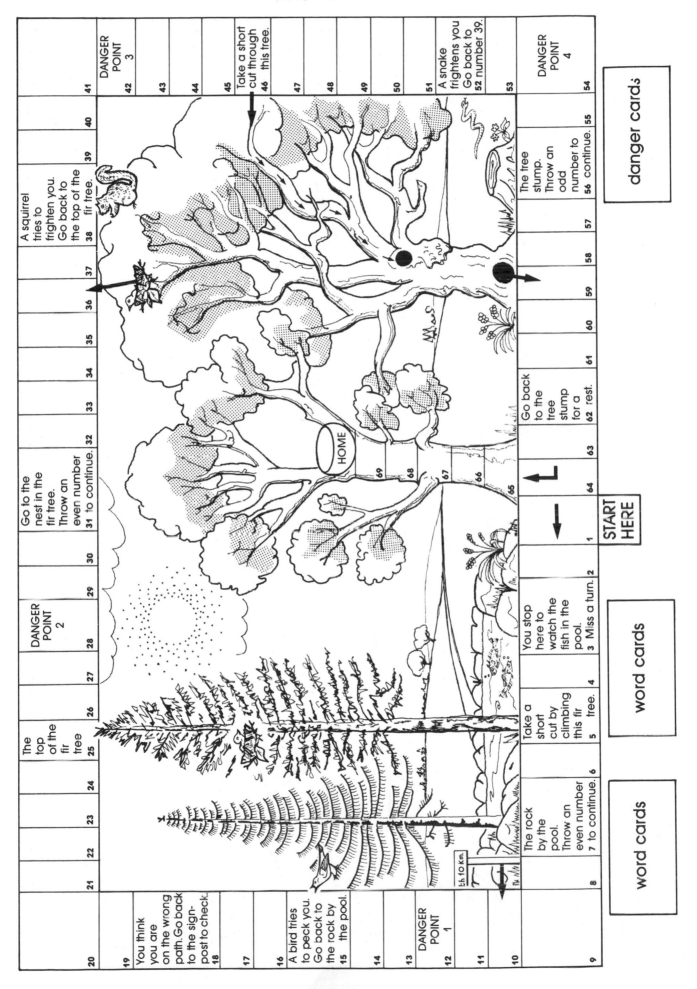

The Forest Trail

danger cards

word cards

word cards

word cards

DANGER POINT 3 — 42

43

44

45

Take a short cut through this tree. — 46

47

48

49

50

51

A snake frightens you. Go back to number 39. — 52

53

DANGER POINT 4 — 54

41

40

39

38 — A squirrel tries to frighten you. Go back to the top of the fir tree.

37

36

35

34

33

32 — Go to the nest in the fir tree. Throw an even number to continue. 31

30

The tree stump. Throw an odd number to continue. — 56

55

57

58

59

60

61

Go back to the tree stump for a rest. — 62

63

64

65

66

67

68

69

HOME

START HERE — 1

2

You stop here to watch the fish in the pool. Miss a turn. — 3

4

Take a short cut by climbing this fir tree. — 5

6 — The rock by the pool. Throw an even number to continue. 7

8

9

10

DANGER POINT 1 — 12

11

13 — DANGER POINT

14

A bird tries to peck you. Go back to the rock by the pool. — 16, 15

17

You think you are on the wrong path. Go back to the sign-post to check. — 18

19

20

21

22

23

24

25 — The top of the fir tree

26

27

DANGER POINT 2 — 28

29

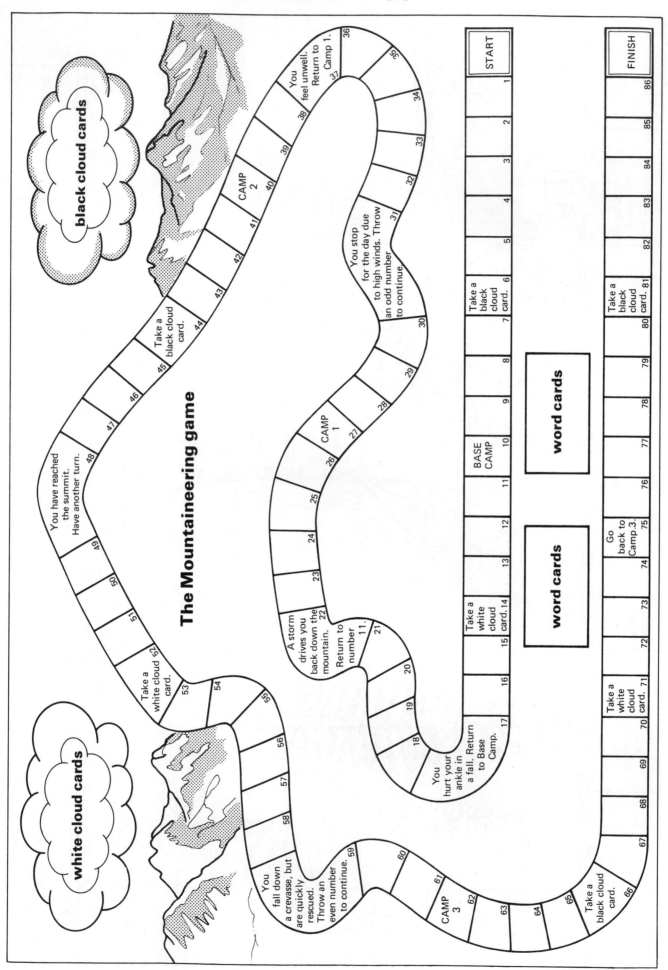

The Mountaineering game

black cloud cards

white cloud cards

word cards

word cards

START 1

FINISH 86

BASE CAMP

CAMP 1

CAMP 2

CAMP 3

Take a black cloud card. 7

Take a black cloud card. 81

Take a white cloud card. 14

Go back to Camp. 3. 75

Take a white cloud card. 71

Take a black cloud card. 44

Take a white cloud card. 53

Take a black cloud card. 66

You feel unwell. Return to Camp 1. 37

You stop for the day due to high winds. Throw an odd number to continue. 31

A storm drives you back down the mountain. Return to number 11. 22

You hurt your ankle in a fall. Return to Base Camp. 17

You have reached the summit. Have another turn. 48

You fall down a crevasse, but are quickly rescued. Throw an even number to continue. 59

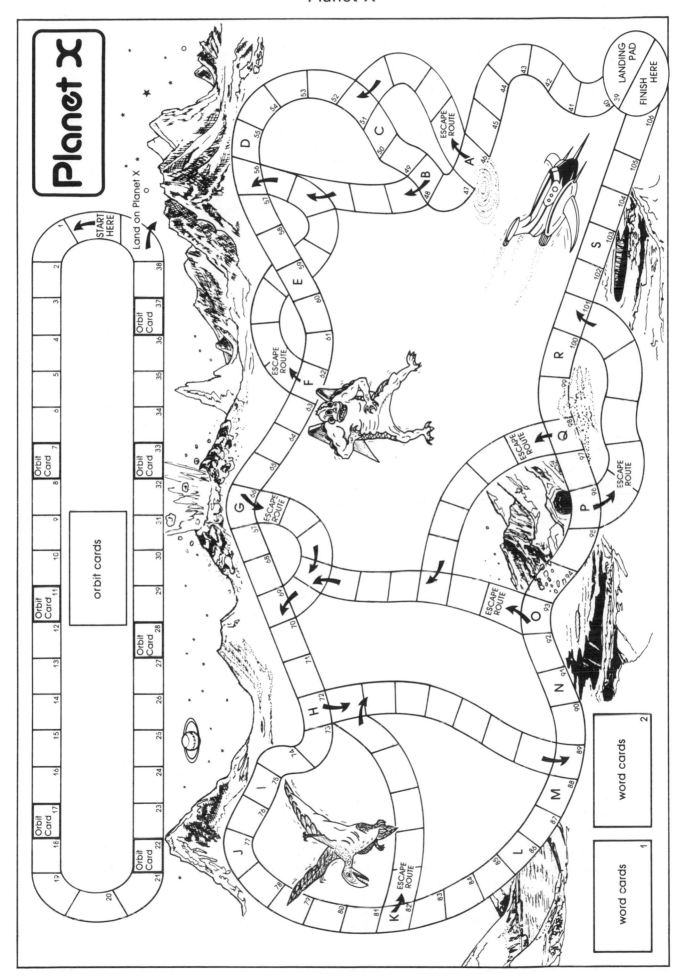

The Tree Game

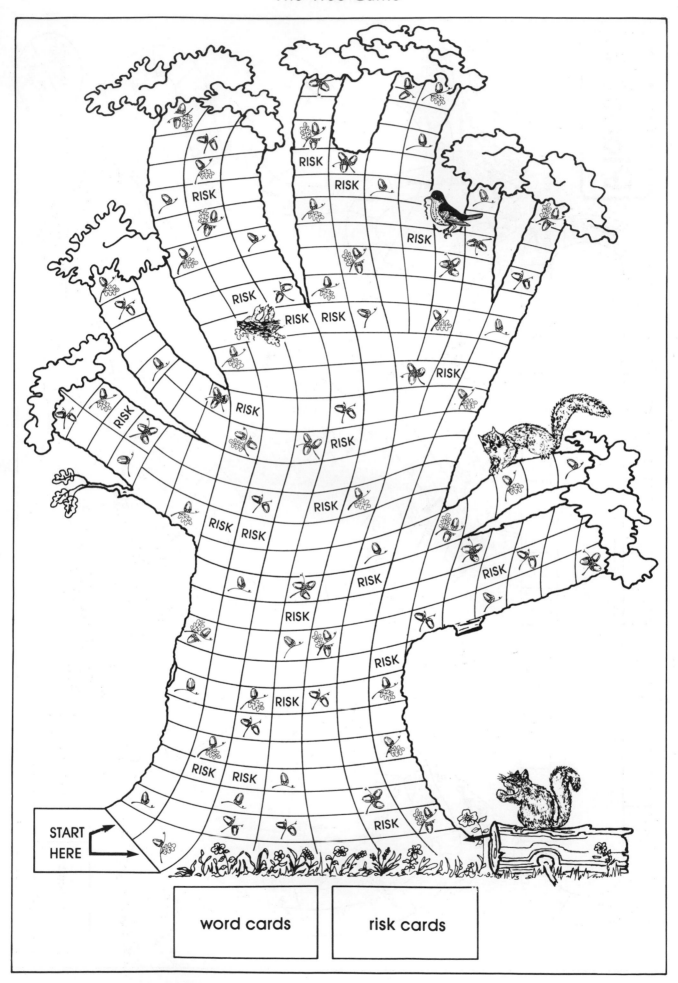

START HERE

word cards

risk cards

Myself

Form ....

Date ....

Your name ....

Your address ....

....

....

Your Junior school ....

When is your birthday? ....

Do you write with your right or your left hand? ....

Do you wear glasses? ....

What colour is your hair? ....

What colour are your eyes? ....

Do you live in a flat or a house? ....

How many brothers do you have? ....

How many sisters do you have? ....

What pets do you have? ....

What are your favourite television programmes? ....

....

Draw yourself and your family, or your pets.

The alphabet (1)*

Here are the small letters.

a b c   d e f   g h i   j k l

m n o   p q r   s t u   v w x

y z

Put in the missing letters.

1

a b _____ d e _____ g h _____ j k _____

m n _____ p q _____ s t _____ v w _____

y _____

2

a _____ c d _____ f g _____ i j _____ l

m _____ o p _____ r s _____ u v _____ x

_____ z

3

_____ b c _____ e f _____ h i _____ k l

_____ n o _____ q r _____ t u _____ w x

_____

The alphabet (2)*

Here are the capital letters.

A B C D E F   G H I J K L
M N O P Q R   S T U V W X
Y Z

---

1 *Put the right capital letters under the small letters.*

a	b	c	d	e	f	g	h	i	j	k	l
A											

m	n	o	p	q	r	s	t	u	v	w	x

y	z

---

2 *Write the small letters here.*

---

3 *Write the capital letters here.*

The alphabet (3)*

---

1   There are <u>26</u> letters in the alphabet.

2   The letters **a**, **e**, **i**, **o**, **u** are called <u>vowels</u>.

3   The other <u>21</u> letters are called <u>consonants</u>.

Write the alphabet in small letters and draw a ring around the <u>5 vowels</u>.

....

....

....

The vowels have <u>2</u> sounds. 1 The long sound. This is the <u>name</u> of the vowel. 2 The short sound.	*Write 2 words with the same vowel sound.*
a in **cat**	....
e in **hen**	....
i in **pig**	....
o in **dog**	....
u in **cup**	....

Vowels — short sound

Put in the **a**		
1	ad	b __ d d __ d h __ d s __ d
2	ag	b __ g r __ g w __ g
3	an	c __ n m __ n n __ n p __ n r __ n v __ n
4	at	b __ t c __ t f __ t h __ t s __ t r __ t

Put in the **e**		
1	ed	b __ d f __ d l __ d r __ d
2	eg	b __ g l __ g p __ g
3	en	h __ n p __ n m __ n
4	et	g __ t l __ t m __ t p __ t w __ t

Put in the **i**		
1	id	d __ d h __ d l __ d
2	ig	b __ g d __ g p __ g
3	ip	h __ p l __ p p __ p
4	it	b __ t f __ t h __ t k __ t s __ t

Put in the **o**		
1	od	c __ d g __ d n __ d r __ d
2	og	d __ g f __ g l __ g
3	op	c __ p h __ p t __ p
4	ot	g __ t h __ t l __ t n __ t

Put in the **u**		
1	ub	c __ b p __ b r __ b t __ b
2	ug	h __ g m __ g r __ g
3	um	g __ m s __ m m __ m
4	ut	b __ t c __ t h __ t

Consonants

A Write a word that begins with the same letter.

1 b as in **bag**	....	12 p as in **pet**	....
2 c as in **cat**	....	13 qu as in **queen**	....
3 d as in **dog**	....	14 r as in **rat**	....
4 f as in **fun**	....	15 s as in **sat**	....
5 g as in **get**	....	16 t as in **top**	....
6 h as in **hit**	....	17 v as in **van**	....
7 j as in **jam**	....	18 w as in **win**	....
8 k as in **kit**	....	*Put the x at the end.* 19 x as in **fox**	....
9 l as in **lip**	....	20 y as in **yes**	....
10 m as in **man**	....	21 z as in **zebra**	....
11 n as in **not**	....		

B Put a letter in front to make a word.

a	e	i	o	u
1	**2**	**3**	**4**	**5**
__ ad	__ et	__ it	__ od	__ un
__ ag	__ eg	__ ip	__ og	__ ub
__ an	__ en	__ in	__ op	__ ut
__ ap	__ ed	__ im	__ ot	__ ug

The note in the bottle*

Jill and John went to the seaside. They ran into the sea and as they came out they found a green bottle on the sand. There was a piece of paper inside the bottle so they took the top off. Inside was a note with a mystery message. Jill and John solved the mystery message. Can you solve it too?

This is what you do:

Read sentence number 1.

Find the letter that is in the first word but not in the second word.

Put that letter in the number 1 box at the end of the message. (The small boxes are for the letters and they make up the big boxes which are the words.)

Find the other letters in the same way.

1   This letter is in **had** but not in **bad**.

2   This letter is in **red** but not in **rod**.

3   This letter is in **let** but not in **net**.

4   This letter is in **pan** but not in **man**.

5   This letter is in **mop** but not in **hop**.

6   This letter is in **yet** but not in **pet**.

7   This letter is in **bit** but not in **fit**.

8   This letter is in **top** but not in **tap**.

9   This letter is in **ham** but not in **him**.

10   This letter is in **hut** but not in **hug**.

11   This letter is in **sat** but not in **hat**.

12   This letter is in **ran** but not in **run**.

13   This letter is in **can** but not in **cat**.

14   This letter is in **kit** but not in **sit**.

15   This letter is in **Ian** but not in **Jan**.

continued on page A8

The note in the bottle

continued from page A7

16   This letter is in **cap** but not in **cup**.

17   This letter is in **mad** but not in **dad**.

18   This letter is in **hot** but not in **got**.

19   This letter is in **leg** but not in **log**.

20   This letter is in **rag** but not in **bag**.

21   This letter is in **pen** but not in **pin**.

			!
1	2	3	4

5	6

7	8	9	10

			.
11	12	13	14

15

16	17

			.
18	19	20	21

Bill Smith

Draw a picture of Bill's island, or of Jill and John finding the bottle.

Basic words (1)*

the	they	are	for	over
this	you	with	from	all
there	her	one	back	some
then	was	said	here	look
that	were	have	come	our

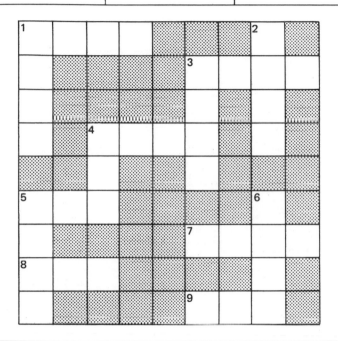

Choose from the words that are underlined.

Clues across

1 'Yes, you can go with her,' Mum s _ _ _ .

3 I do not have that mug, I have th _ _ one.

4 'Come over h _ _ _ ,' said Dad.

5 I went to look f _ _ my dog.

7 'Can I h _ _ _ a cup of milk?' I said.

8 'Get me o _ _ tin of ham,' said Mum.

9 I like ou _ cat to sit on my lap.

Clues down

1 Here are s _ _ _ red pens.

2 'Will you come w _ _ _ me?' said Tom.

3 Pat and Sam went to the park and t _ _ _ came back at four pm.

4 Jill cut h _ _ leg.

5 I had a big bag f _ _ _ my Dad for Xmas.

6 Our cat will not sit on the rug. She jumps o _ _ _ it.

Basic words (2)*

must	she	only	call	put
just	their	before	when	could
much	your	after	what	again
very	any	now	where	want
every	out	down	which	because
			first	right

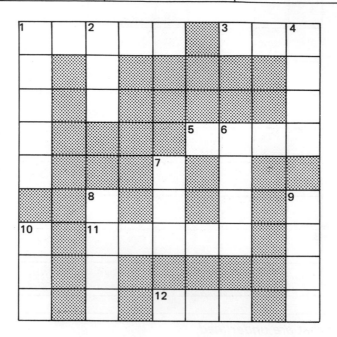

Choose from the words that are underlined.

Clues across

1 Do that sum a _ _ _ _ .

3 My mother said, 'Come here n _ _ .'

5 Put the pen d _ _ _ on the desk.

11 I like e _ _ _ _ one.

12 Get your P.E. kit o _ _ of your bag.

Clues down

1 I will go out a _ _ _ _ tea.

2 'Have you a _ _ big eggs?' I said.

4 Wh _ _ will you come to see me?

6 There is o _ _ _ one rod left.

7 My mother said that sh _ felt ill.

8 It is v _ _ _ hot in here.

9 'Wh _ _ do you want?' I said.

10 I will p _ _ on a hat because it is very cold.

Word endings (1)*

nd	nk	ng	nt
band	bank	bang	ant
hand	sank	rang	rent
land	tank	ring	sent
sand	sink	sing	tent
send	pink	long	went
wind	bunk	song	pint
find	sunk	lung	hunt

Choose from the words that are underlined.

Clues across

1 You find s _ _ _ by the sea.

3 I can sing a s _ _ _ _ .

6 When we go camping we have a big

t _ _ _ .

8 Every Sunday the b _ _ _ plays in

the park.

10 The w _ _ _ is very cold today.

12 I have a big fish in my fish t _ _ _ .

13 My father cut his h _ _ _ today.

Clues down

1 My mother s _ _ _ me to get a tin of beans.

2 My dog has very l _ _ _ legs.

4 I could not f _ _ _ my pen.

5 There was a big a _ _ on my leg.

7 I r _ _ _ the bell but Tom was not in.

9 My father has a job in the b _ _ _ .

10 On Sunday I w _ _ _ out with Ann.

11 I did not like the bag but they said I could s _ _ _ it back.

Word endings (2)*

ft	ld	mp	different endings
1	**2**	**3**	**4**
raft	held	camp	myself
left	hold	damp	help
gift	cold	lamp	film
lift	gold	bump	milk
loft	sold	lump	felt
soft	told	pump	kept

Complete each sentence by using the right word from the box at the side.

1	I have a .... bed.	myself soft	loft bump
2	I had a big tent when I went to	damp lamp	cold camp
3	I have a cup of .... before I go to bed.	lift felt	milk left
4	I went to see a .... on Saturday.	gift bump	milk film
5	My mother had to .... me do my sums.	held help	kept lamp
6	I fell over and now I have a big .... on my leg.	gift pump	lump damp
7	I have a very bad	hold cold	gold camp
8	My father has .... his car.	soft told	hold sold
9	I .... my P.E. kit at home.	lift raft	left held
10	I .... ill and had to go home.	left loft	felt film
11	I could not .... my mug of tea because it was very hot.	sold help	cold hold

Short and long vowels;   silent e*

1 short vowels	2 long vowels *Add an e to make the vowel say its own name.*

a

1	at	ate
2	can	can __
3	hat	hat __
4	mad	mad __
5	mat	mat __
6	man	man __
7	tap	tap __

3 short vowels	4 long vowels *Add an e to make the vowel say its own name.*

i

1	bit	bite
2	hid	hid __
3	kit	kit __
4	pin	pin __
5	pip	pip __
6	rid	rid __
7	rip	rip __
8	win	win __

o

1	cod	code
2	hop	hop __
3	not	not __
4	rod	rod __

u

1	cub	cube
2	tub	tub __
3	us	us __

a + e; silent e*

*The a says its own name (long sound) and the e is silent. When you see * say the c like the s in sit.*

1	2	3	4	5
*face	cake	sale	lane	gate
*race	lake	came	mane	hate
made	make	game	ape	late
safe	take	name	tape	mate
age	wake	same	base	cave
cage	male	tame	case	gave
page	female	cane	ate	save
bake	pale	pane	date	wave

A Complete each sentence by putting the words at the side in the right order.

1 If I wake up late I have to run to school because I ....
....
   to   be
   hate   late.

2 My dog's name is Dan. He has ....
.... my friend.
   the   as
   same   name

3 I made a cage for my tame mice. The male is black and the ....
....
   is   pale
   female   grey.

4 I said to my mother, 'Will you ....
.... the same as the one we had on Sunday?'
   bake   a
   date   cake,

5 Jane said that it was not safe to ....
....
   into   go
   cave.   the

6 I take my dog for a walk to ....
....
   lake   the
   every   day.

7 I am very ....
   tall   my
   for   age.

B Put each word in a sentence: (1) make (2) name (3) gave.

....
....
....

Short and long vowels; ai; silent i*

	short a	long a
		Add an i to make the a say its own name.
1	am	a __ m
2	bat	ba __ t
3	man	ma __ n
4	pad	pa __ d
5	pan	pa __ n
6	pant	pa __ nt
7	ran	ra __ n

A Say the name of each picture. Draw a ring around its name.

tail mail	raid hail
pail nail	sail wait

rail tail	aim pain
bait main	rain paint

sail pail	nail wait
gain jail	paint aid

B Put each word in a sentence: (1) pain (2) sail (3) wait.

....

....

....

ai and ay*

The a usually says its own name (long sound) and the i and the y are silent.				
ai				ay
1	2	3	4	5
aid	nail	gain	*Say the air like the air in* chair.	day
laid	pail	main		today
paid	rail	pain		hay
raid	sail	paint		lay
fail	tail	rain	air	may
hail	aim	vain	fair	pay
jail		bait	hair	ray
mail		wait	pair	say
			chair	way
			stairs	always

Put the right word in the box at the side.

Choose from these words:

nail	rain	sail	May	jail
pain	chair	tail	bait	stairs

1	Which one do you put up in a boat?	....
2	Which one do you feel when you hurt yourself?	....
3	Which one is a month of the year?	....
4	Which one can make you wet?	....
5	Which one do you put on a hook at the end of a fishing line to help you catch fish?	....
6	Which one is another name for prison?	....
7	Which one grows on the end of a finger?	....
8	Which one do you sit on?	....
9	Which one does a dog wag?	....
10	Which one do you go up to get to the next floor?	....

Short and long vowels; **ea**; silent **a**

short **e**	long **e** *Add an **a** to make the* *e say its own name.*
1 Ben	be __ n
2 bet	be __ t
3 led	le __ d
4 Len	le __ n
5 men	me __ n
6 net	ne __ t
7 red	re __ d
8 set	se __ t

A   Say the name of each picture. Draw a ring around its name.

tea sea	read load
eat pea	real lean
heat meat	leak team
neat seat	leaf leap
beak bean	meal mean
beat weak	beam jeans

B   Put each word in a sentence: (1) eat   (2) tea   (3) jeans.

....

....

....

ea*

The **e** usually says its own name (long sound) and the **a** is silent.				Say the **ear** in these words like the word **ear**.
1	**2**	**3**	**4**	**5**
pea	beak	seam	leap	dear
sea	leak	team	eat	fear
tea	weak	bean	beat	gear
lead	deal	lean	heat	hear
read	heal	mean	meat	near
leaf	meal	jeans	neat	tear
	real		seat	year

A What am I?   Change the first letter of the old word to make a new word that fits the new meaning.

old word	new meaning	new word
1 tea	You can swim in me.	....
2 read	You fix me to a dog's collar.	....
3 leak	I am the bill of a bird.	....
4 deal	I mean to get better: the cut on your ear will soon	....
5 bean	I mean having very little fat.	....
6 real	I am food: when you are hungry you eat a big	....
7 meat	I mean very tidy.	....
8 heat	You can sit on me.	....
9 hear	I mean close by.	....
10 gear	I am the feeling you have when you are afraid.	....

B Put the two words in the box in a sentence.

1	....	year sea
2	....	team beat

ee

The first **e** usually says its own name (long sound) and the second **e** is silent.

1	2	3	4
bee	beef	been	seem
see	week	seen	feet
feed	feel	deep	meet
need	heel	jeep	*Say the* **ee** *in these words like the word* **ear**.
seed	peel	keep	beer
weed	reel	weep	deer

A   What am I?   Change the first letter of the old word to make a new word that fits the new meaning.

old word		new meaning	new word
1	meet	You put shoes on me.	....
2	feel	I am the skin of an apple.	....
3	weed	A new plant grows from me.	....
4	jeep	I mean a long way down: the water in the lake is very	....
5	reel	I am the back of the feet.	....
6	keep	I mean to cry.	....
7	need	I mean to give food to.	....
8	been	I am the past tense of the word see: have you .... the film at the Odeon?	....
9	deer	I am sold in a pub.	....

Add a letter to the end of the next word.

10	bee	I am the meat from a cow.	....

B   Put the two words in the box in a sentence.

1	....	meet week
2	....	feet feel

The message; ea and ee*

> **A**   The message is in code. Find out what it says. Put a capital letter after a full stop, for the word I, and for names.

The code:

1	2	3	4	5	6	7	8	9	10	11	12	13
a	b	c	d	e	f	g	h	i	j	k	l	m

14	15	16	17	18	19	20	21	22	23	24	25	26
n	o	p	q	r	s	t	u	v	w	x	y	z

The Message

16 5 20 5

....

        23 5   19 8 1 12 12   13 5 5 20   14 5 24 20

23 5 5 11   9 14   20 8 5   13 5 1 14   13 1 14

3 1 6 5   6 15 18   1   13 5 1 12 •   25 15 21

23 9 12 12   19 5 5   20 8 5   11 5 25 19   15 6

20 8 5   10 5 5 16   15 14   15 14 5   15 6   20 8 5

19 5 1 20 19 •   11 5 5 16   20 15   20 8 5   19 5 1

18 15 1 4   20 8 5 14   20 21 18 14   12 5 6 20   1 20

12 5 1 6   12 1 14 5 •   20 8 9 19   12 1 14 5

12 5 1 4 19   20 15   20 8 5   3 1 6 5 •   20 8 5 18 5

9 19   14 15   14 5 5 4   20 15   6 5 1 18   2 5 14 •

8 5   9 19   23 5 1 11   1 14 4   9   23 9 12 12

4 5 1 12   23 9 20 8   8 9 13 •

        20 5 1 13   12 5 1 4 5 18

> **B**   Put each word in a sentence: (1) sea   (2) see   (3) meet.

The short and long sound of **a** and **e**

> *The vowel in the first word has a short sound.*
> *The vowel in the second word says its own name (long sound).*

Put the words at the side in the right spaces.

1 Tom got .... when he was .... to go to bed at nine o'clock.	mad made
2 I .... all the way home in the	ran rain
3 I .... my mother's red	hat hate
4 .... has the .... make of bike as I have.	Sam same
5 The .... went to the .... line station to catch a train.	man main
6 I put some .... on the .... to stop the leak.	tap tape
7 I .... my friend 50p that I would .... him in the race.	bet beat
8 I .... my dog on his red .... in the park.	led lead
9 My sister likes me to .... her the story of the little .... hen.	red read
10 I .... my mother near the shops and she said she was going to buy some .... for dinner.	met meat

Silent e; i + e*

The i *says its own name (long sound) and the* e *is silent.* When you see *say the c *like the* s *in* sit.				

i + e

1	2	3	4	5
*ice	beside	tile	vine	bite
*dice	wide	lime	wine	kite
*mice	life	mime	pipe	site
*nice	wife	time	ripe	dive
*rice	bike	fine	rise	five
*vice	like	line	wise	live
hide	file	mine	fire	(also lĭve)
ride	mile	nine	hire	alive
side	pile	pine	wire	wives
				size

Complete each sentence by using the right words from the box at the side.	
1 I live .... away from school.	fine file miles five
2 I ate a .... apple for tea.	nice ride nine ripe
3 My brother's wife told me it was .... to .... to work on my bike.	tile ride time side
4 My sister's .... and .... look alike.	bite bike mime mine
5 The Woodwork teacher told us how to use a .... and a	vice fire vine file
6 As we are a big family we .... a car to take us to the sea .... for our holidays.	site wire side hire
7 I take .... five in shoes. I like them to be very	wise size wide beside
8 On Friday my five pet .... were .... but then two died suddenly in the night.	wives mice alive rice

Silent e; i + e

A Can you read the story below? Before you try you will have to complete the words with spaces in them so that it makes sense.

Choose from these words:

beside	like	nice	nine	wise	lines	ride (2)	fine
wide	dive (2)	wine	ice	bikes	Pine	bite	site
mile	time	pile	five	sunshine	side		

PICNIC AT PINE TREE LAKE

It was a f _ _ _ Sunday and the sun _ _ _ _ _ _ made us feel l _ _ _ a picnic. So at n _ _ _ o'clock Tom and I went for a r _ _ _ on our b _ _ _ _ by the s _ _ _ of P _ _ _ Tree Lake which is f _ _ _ miles long and a m _ _ _ w _ _ _ . It is very beautiful.

At ten o'clock we saw a nic _ s _ _ _ for a picnic. So we sat in the sun be _ _ _ _ the lake and had a p _ _ _ of sandwiches and some w _ _ _ .

Tom said, 'Let's d _ _ _ into the lake. I'm very hot'. 'No,' I replied. 'It isn't wi _ _ to d _ _ _ into cold water after a big meal.'

So we got out our fishing l _ _ _ _ and sat on the bank to wait for the fish to b _ _ _. But we were unlucky.

At five o'clock it was t _ _ _ to r _ _ _ home. We had a lemon i _ _ on the way home and we both agreed it had been a very happy day.

B Draw one of the following: (1) a picture of the story (2) the fish in the lake
(3) fishing gear — line, reel, etc.

Silent e; o + e

The o usually says its own name (long sound) and the e is silent.				The o in these words has a different sound.
1 code rode coke joke poke woke	**2** dole hole mole pole sole home	**3** bone cone tone hope Pope rope	**4** hose nose rose note vote doze	**5** more sore tore gone

Say the o like the oo in moon.

move

A Put the right word in the spaces. Change the first letter of the old word to make a new word that will make sense in the sentence.

old word	
1 code	Last week I .... to school on my bike.
2 joke	I like to drink ....
3 poke	I was late for school because I .... up at nine o'clock.
4 rose	You smell with your ....
5 hope	We tied up the boat with a ....
6 vote	When I am ill my mother always sends a .... to my teacher.
7 more	I fell off my bike today and now I have a .... leg.
8 cone	My dog likes a nice meaty ....
9 dole	I tore my jumper and now there is a big .... in it.

B Put each word in a sentence: (1) home (2) rode (3) gone.

....

....

....

oa

The **o** usually says its own name (long sound) and the **a** is silent.			The **oa** in these words has a different sound.
1	**2**	**3**	**4**
load	coal	soap	oar
road	foal	boat	roar
toad	goal	coat	board
loaf	loan	goat	broad
oak	moan	moat	abroad
soak	foam	oats	
			cupboard

A   Complete each sentence using the right word from the box at the side.

		coal soak
1	I paid £20 for a	coat toad

		loan coal
2	I like to see a nice .... fire.	foal load

		soap road
3	The teacher said, 'Come in, this rain will .... you.'	oak soak

		soak goal
4	My mother says, 'Always use .... when you wash your hands.'	soap foam

		toad moan
5	We live in a very long	load road

		broad board
6	I want to go .... to Spain for my holiday.	abroad boat

		goat coal
7	Our netball team won by one .... to nil.	moat goal

		loan loaf
8	My mother told me to get a .... of bread.	oar oats

		board abroad
9	I put our cups in the	cupboard roar

B   Put each word in a sentence: (1) road   (2) coat   (3) boat.

....

....

....

o + e and oa crossword

Choose from these words:

rope	home	woke
sole	hole	pole
oak	note	toad
nose	loaf	goal
road	moan	soap
coal	rose	

Clues across

1 My dog always digs a _ _ _ _ for

his bones.

3 I tied up the boat with a _ _ _ _ .

5 I always _ _ _ _ when I have to

see the dentist.

6 At the seaside I cut the _ _ _ _ of my foot on a tin can.

9 My mother left a _ _ _ _ for the milkman saying 'No milk today'.

11 My father said that I was not to play in the _ _ _ _ .

12 I always wash my face with _ _ _ _ and water.

14 On Friday we went to bed late and _ _ _ _ up late.

Clues down

1 I felt ill in school and was sent _ _ _ _ .

2 We cut up a _ _ _ _ of bread for our picnic.

3 A _ _ _ _ is a flower.

4 It is very cold at the north _ _ _ _ .

7 My team beat 2S one _ _ _ _ to nil.

8 My mother says she likes a nice _ _ _ _ fire.

9 You smell with your _ _ _ _ .

10 A _ _ _ _ is like a frog.

13 Our chairs are made of _ _ _ .

Silent e; u + e

The **u** says its own name (long sound) and the **e** is silent.			
1 cube tube huge duke	**2** juke-box mule fumes June tune	**3** use cute cure pure sure	**4** *Say the **u** in these words like the **oo** in **moon**.* rude rule

Write a sentence about each picture. Put the word or words in the box in your sentence.
Colour the pictures.

Picture	Sentence	Words
	....	two cubes glass
	....	tube brush
	....	huge dragon
	....	fumes car
	....	cure cold
	....	sister cute brother rude
	....	tunes juke-box dance
	....	queen rules
	....	roses June flower

u + e crossword

Choose from these words:

duke	rude	June
juke-box	tunes	tube
huge	cure	cube
use	fuse	sure

Clues across

2 The sixth month of the year is J _ _ _ .

4 A duchess is the wife of a d _ _ _ .

5 We play the same t _ _ _ _ over and

over again on the juke-box.

9 Dad told me not to u _ _ his pen.

10 My mother gave me some tablets to c _ _ _ my bad cold.

Clues down

1 It is r _ _ _ not to say please and thank you.

2 The j _ _ _ - _ _ _ in the café has many up-to-date tunes.

3 I had a very big meal in the café. It was so h _ _ _ that I felt ill.

5 I had to buy a t _ _ _ of toothpaste.

6 Mum said, 'Are you s _ _ _ that you want to see the film at the Odeon?'

7 I take one c _ _ _ of sugar in my tea.

8 All electric plugs have a f _ _ _ .

Write three sentences. See how many u + e words you can use.

....

....

....

....

The short and the long sound of **i**, **o** and **u**

The vowel in the first word has a short sound. The vowel in the second word says its own name.

Put the words at the side in the right spaces.

1 I told my brother to .... and he .... behind the cupboard.	hid hide
2 .... fell off his bike and cut the .... of his face.	Sid side
3 Mum said to me, 'Get .... of that sad face. Go for a .... on your bike to make you feel better.'	rid ride
4 My father gave me a .... to make a big	kit kite
5 'I .... you win the .... , skip and jump race,' said Dad.	hop hope
6 'I will .... give you a .... saying you are ill,' said Mum.	not note
7 I got my fishing .... out of the cupboard and .... to the lake on my bike.	rod rode
8 I gave my father a .... when I met him.	hug huge
9 I went to see the bear .... at the zoo. The keeper gave all of them two .... of sugar.	cubs cubes
10 The P.E. teacher told .... that we could not .... the gym.	us use

r blends*

br	cr	dr	fr	gr	pr	tr
1	**2**	**3**	**4**	**5**	**6**	**7**
brain	crab	dream	free	grab	pram	train
brake	cream	dress	freeze	grapes	pray	trap
brave	croak	drink	frog	green	press	tree
bride	crops	drive	from	grin	price	trunk
bring	cross	drop	fruit	grip	print	true
broke	cry	dry	fry	groan	prize	try

True or false (untrue)?	answer
1 Grapes are a fruit.	true
2 The opposite of dry is drop.	....
3 Crabs live in the sea.	....
4 All tree-trunks are brown.	....
5 When water freezes it becomes ice.	....
6 Your brain is in your head.	....
7 A grin is a wide smile.	....
8 You always fry eggs in a kettle.	....
9 Frogs croak.	....
10 Trains run on rails.	....
11 You can buy an orange drink from a bank.	....
12 In Britain we drive on the left-hand side of the road.	....

l blends

bl	cl	fl	gl	pl	sl
1	**2**	**3**	**4**	**5**	**6**
black	clap	flag	glad	plan	slam
blame	clean	flat	gleam	plane	slap
blanket	cliff	flame	glide	plate	slave
bleed	clock	float	globe	play	sleep
blind	close	fleet	glue	please	slide
blond	club	fly		plot	slip
blue	clue			plum	slim

Complete each sentence by putting the words at the side in the right order.

1	Mum said,'I'm glad your	dress	is
		clean.'	black
2	When you come in please close the door	don't	slam
		but	it.
3	You can see that the world is not flat when you	at	look
		a	globe.
4	The slim girl had blue eyes	and	hair.
		blond	long
5	I was ill after I ate	plate	a
		of	plums.
6	Last year we went to Spain by car. This year we	going	are
		plane.	by
7	I saw a blind man	slip on	the
		wet	road.
8	I like to go to	sleep	ten
		o'clock.	before
9	In winter I always have two	on	blankets
		bed.	my

s blends*

sp	sc	sk	sm	sn	st	sw
1	**2**	**3**	**4**	**5**	**6**	**7**
spell	scab	skin	smell	snap	stop	swim
spend	scalp	skid	smile	sniff	step	swing
spill	scales	skip	smoke	snake	still	swop
spin	scone	skill		snail	stamp	sweep
spot	escape	skull		sneeze	stand	sweet
spy	rescue	sky			stay	
speak		skate			lost	
spoke		desk			must	
speed		risk			just	

Complete each sentence using the right word or words from the box at the side.

1	I spend all my pocket money on	stand stamps skin must
2	When I have a cold I seem to .... and .... all day.	snail sniff sneeze still
3	I like .... and .... stories best.	scales scalp escape spy
4	The .... was very black and big .... of rain began to fall.	spots desk skull sky
5	When I go to the seaside I like to .... in the sea.	swing sweet rescue swim
6	I don't like the .... of coal	smile smell skill smoke
7	My mother's scales are broken but she .... made .... for us.	scones spoke spill still
8	I .... my English book on the way home yesterday.	just stay swop lost
9	My father said that I .... not .... when I am eating.	spin must speed speak
10	I had to .... at home yesterday because I had a cold.	spell stay stand snap

Crossword; r, l and s blends

Choose from these words:

fry	globe	cry	clock
lost	plate	bring	green
bride	brakes	grin	please
cross	stamp	price	slap
skull	flag	plane	sleep
snake	sky	fly	dry

Clues across

1 You must always br _ _ _ your P.E. kit for the P.E. lesson.

3 A gl _ _ _ is a complete map of the world.

6 My mother said that the pr _ _ _ of cream is very high.

7 I always dr _ the plates.

8 I kept very still as the green grass sn _ _ _ slid past.

9 My father was very cross when I spoke rudely to my mother and he gave me a sl _ _ .

12 In winter my black cat goes to sl _ _ p all day.

14 My mother was cr _ _ _ when I broke a plate.

15 My fl _ flew into the spider's web.

16 The British fl _ _ is red, white and blue.

17 I went by pl _ _ _ to Sweden this year.

18 The bony frame of the head is called the sk _ _ _ .

Clues down

1 I could not stop my bike at the crossroads because its br _ _ _ _ were bad. I had a lucky escape.

2 Another name for a smile is a gr _ _ .

3 Some frogs are brown and some are gr _ _ _ .

4 The br _ _ _ wore a long, white dress.

5 On Sunday I fr _ bacon and eggs for breakfast.

6 If you ask for something you must always say pl _ _ _ _ .

8 There are nine planets in the sk _ . (Can you name them?)

10 Our address is on a disc on our dog's collar, so that he does not get l _ st.

11 I always cr _ if a film is sad.

12 The first penny black st _ _ _ was used on 1st May 1840.

13 My dog was so hungry that he ate his pl _ _ _ of meat in twenty seconds.

14 I was late for school today because the cl _ _ _ had stopped at eight o'clock.

sh*

Say the **sh** *like the* **sh** *in* **fish**.

short vowel	long vowel	short vowel
1	**2**	**3**
shall	shade	ash
<u>shed</u>	shake	<u>cash</u>
shelf	shape	dish
<u>shell</u>	shave	<u>fish</u>
shift	<u>sheep</u>	wish
<u>ship</u>	<u>sheet</u>	rush
<u>shop</u>	shine	crash
shot	<u>shoal</u>	flash
<u>shut</u>	show	smash
		<u>push</u>

What am I?   Put the right word in the box at the side.
Choose from the words that are underlined.

clues	answers
1 You can find me on the beach at the seaside.	....
2 I am the opposite of open.	....
3 I am alive and you find me in the sea and in rivers.	....
4 You can ride on the sea in me.	....
5 You buy things with me.	....
6 You buy things in me.	....
7 I mean many fish swimming together.	....
8 You get wool from me.	....
9 When you make the bed you put me on the bed before you put the blanket on.	....
10 I am a small hut.	....
11 I mean to press.	....

ch

Say the **ch** like the **ch** in **church**.

short vowel	long vowel	short vowel	long vowel
1	**2**	**3**	**4**
chat	chain	rich	each
chest	change	much	beach
chill	chase	such	peach
chin	cheap	bench	reach
chips	cheek	bunch	teach
chop	cheese	lunch	teacher
check	choke		
children	child		church

What am I? Put the right word in the box at the side.
Choose from the words that are underlined.

	clues	answers
1	There is one of me on each side of your face.	....
2	You often eat me with fish.	....
3	I am the name of the meal you eat between 12 o'clock and 2 o'clock.	....
4	Mice like me very much.	....
5	A bike will not go without me.	....
6	I mean having a lot of money.	....
7	I teach in a school.	....
8	I am a fruit. My name rhymes with reach.	....
9	I am the opposite of expensive (dear).	....
10	I am the sandy or pebbly shore of the sea.	....
11	Teachers teach me in school.	....
12	I mean to run after.	....

sh and ch crossword

Choose from these words:

shelf	sheep	crash	shut
church	she	fish	cheese
lunch	shed	shy	ash
each	shop	chop	teach
sh			

Clues across

1 Do not leave the gate open, always

s _ _ _ it.

4 Many people go to c _ _ _ _ _ to

pray to God.

5 Cross off the **r** in the word **reach** and you have the word _ _ _ _ .

7 My mother says that she likes to eat a nice c _ _ _ for dinner.

8 This is not a word. It is the first two letters of the word **shape**, _ _ .

9 My mother and father say they will t _ _ _ _ me to swim.

12 We do not keep my bike in the house; we keep it in the garden s _ _ _ .

13 Today I am going to take my new fishing rod and f _ _ _ in the lake.

14 My brother does not say much as he is very s _ _ .

Clues down

1 My teacher said that wool comes from the coat of a s _ _ _ _ .

2 I had cheese sandwiches for my l _ _ _ _ today.

3 I went to the sweet-s _ _ _ to buy some ice-cream.

6 Butter and c _ _ _ _ _ are made from milk.

8 My mother puts the sweets on the top s _ _ _ _ so that my sister can't reach them.

10 We had a c _ _ _ _ in our car on Sunday.

11 My mother always tells my father not to drop his cigarette a _ _ on the floor.

12 My aunt lives in America and s _ _ is very rich.

tch*

When you see **tch** at the end or in the middle of a word, you only say the **ch**, like the **ch** in **church**.

Put in the **a**	Put in the **a**	Put in the **e**	Put in the **i**	Put in the **o**	Put in the **u**
1	**2**	**3**	**4**	**5**	**6**
b__tch	sn__tch	f__tch	d__tch	sc__tch	D__tch
c__tch	scr__tch	k__tch	h__tch	n__tch	h__tch
h__tch	th__tch	sk__tch	k__tchen		cl__tch
l__tch	str__tch	str__tch	p__tch		cr__tch
m__tch	w__tch		st__tch		
p__tch			sw__tch		b__tcher
disp__tch			w__tch		
s__tchel			__tch		

Complete each sentence by putting the words at the side in the right order.

1	I could not reach the book on the shelf so I had to	up stretch it. for
2	Dad told Keith to put the rabbit	back hutch. the in
3	We do not have a dining room so we	in kitchen. eat the
4	My mother put a plaster on my hand but she said, 'It's	small only scratch.' a
5	I told my dog	to stick. the fetch
6	He looked at his .... the time.	find out watch to
7	'Will you .... I throw it to you?' I said to my sister.	catch when ball the
8	The car	skidded the into ditch.
9	I tore my jeans and my mother had to .... the hole.	a patch stick over

ch saying k*

ch does not always sound like the ch in church.
Sometimes it has the sound of the k in kite.

Words that are often used.		Difficult words: your teacher will help you to read them and you can come back to them later.	
1	**2**	**3**	**4**
school	choir	technology	scheme
Christmas	orchestra	architect	schooner
Christ	chorus	bronchitis	architecture
Christian	echo	chrysalis	archaeology
stomach	chemical	chronic	archaeologist
ache	chemist	chronicle	psychology
character	chemistry	chord	psychologist
anchor	mechanic	chlorine	technique
chaos	mechanical	chromium	
	technical		

Complete the words in the sentences. Choose from the words that are underlined.

1 I was sent home from s _ _ _ _ _ because I had a very bad st _ _ _ _ _ _ a _ _ _

during the chem _ _ _ _ _ lesson.

2 My friend is in the school ch _ _ _ and I am playing the violin in the school

orch _ _ _ _ _ _ . We are rehearsing for the Christ _ _ _ concert. I am also the main

char _ _ _ _ _ in the school play.

3 My father wants me to do something mech _ _ _ _ _ _ when I leave school,

like working as a motor mech _ _ _ _ _ . However, I want to be an archi _ _ _ _

and I am going to take G.C.E. Tech _ _ _ _ _ _ Drawing and Design

and Tech _ _ _ _ _ _ _ .

4 Before I did my homework I had to go to the ch _ _ _ _ _ _ 's to get my mother some

medicine for her bron _ _ _ _ _ _ _ .

5 Last year, during a very bad storm, the Chem _ _ _ _ _ _ lab. ceiling collapsed. There

was ch _ _ s in the room but no one was hurt.

6 The wind was so strong that the boat's an _ _ _ _ _ broke.

ch saying k*

What is the word?   Write the word that fits the meaning.

Choose from the words below.

anchor	choir	mechanic	echo	architect	chemical
chaos	ache	stomach	character	orchestra	Christmas
chemist	schooner	Christian	chrysalis	scheme	

	meaning	answer
1	A part of the body that receives and digests food.	
2	A dull pain.	
3	A person in a story or play.	
4	A ship's mooring. This stops a ship moving.	
5	This word means disorder and confusion.	
6	A company of singers who are trained to sing together.	
7	A group of musicians with instruments.	
8	A sound that is repeated by being thrown back.	
9	A person skilled in chemistry. Also the name of the person you take your prescription to.	
10	A substance used in chemistry.	
11	This is the festival of the birth of Christ. We celebrate it on 25th December.	
12	A man who does skilled work on machinery.	
13	A believer in the religion of Christ. It can also mean your first name.	
14	A kind of sailing ship.	
15	A person who designs buildings.	
16	The form taken by a caterpillar while it is changing into a butterfly or moth.	
17	This means a plan for doing something. It also means to plan in an underhand or secret way.	

ch saying sh*

Sometimes **ch** has the sound of the **sh** in ship.

1	2	3
chef	chassis	chauffeur
chalet	brochure	champagne
machine	chute	avalanche
machinery	parachute	moustache

A   What am I?   Put the letters of the words at the side in the right order.

		clues	answers
1	letcha	I am a small wooden cottage. Sometimes I am built on the sea front.	....
2	fech	I am the head cook.	....
3	moutaches	I am the hair above the top lip.	....
4	chauffreu	I am the paid driver of a motor car.	....
5	chutepara	You have to wear me if you jump from an aircraft in mid-air.	....
6	assisch	I am the main frame of a motor car.	....
7	achinem	Some people sew their clothes by hand and some use me.	....
8	brochrue	I am the name given to a booklet, like the one that advertises holidays.	....
9	ampchagne	I am a sparkling white wine.	....
10	lancheava	I am a mass of snow, ice and rocks falling down a mountain.	....

B   Put each word in a sentence: (1) chef   (2) machine   (3) moustache.

....

....

....

th*

Can you hear the difference between the **th** in columns **1** and **2** and the **th** in columns **3** and **4**?			
th *voiced*		**th** *voiceless*	
1	**2**	**3**	**4**
<u>this</u>	those	<u>thank</u>	<u>thirteen</u>
<u>then</u>	with	<u>thick</u>	Thursday
there	<u>other</u>	thin	birthday
<u>their</u>	<u>mother</u>	thing	<u>both</u>
that	<u>brother</u>	<u>something</u>	<u>bath</u>
than	<u>father</u>	<u>anything</u>	path
<u>they</u>	breathe	nothing	cloth
these	<u>clothes</u>	<u>think</u>	teeth

A   Complete the words with spaces in them. Choose from the words that are underlined.

Today is Th _ _ _ _ _ _ 30th October. It is my bir _ _ _ _ _ and I am

th _ _ _ _ _ _ years old. I have had a lot of presents. My m _ _ _ _ _ and f _ _ _ _ _ _

bo _ _ gave me money for some cl _ _ _ _ _ ; th _ _ always give me money. Th _ _ my

br _ _ _ _ _ gave me a _ _ _ ck winter jumper and my sister gave me some b _ _ _ oil.

My aunt and uncle, who live in America, have sent me s _ _ _ _ _ _ _ _ but it hasn't

arrived yet. Th _ _ r present never arrives in time for my b _ _ _ _ _ _ _ .

My o _ _ er aunt hasn't sent me any _ _ _ _ _ th _ s year but my mother th _ _ _ s

my present has been delayed in the post.

I had too many presents to list but I sent a th _ _ _ you note to everyone.

B   Put each word in a sentence: (1) with (2) things (3) thank (4) birthday (5) clothes.

....

....

....

....

....

wh*

1	2	3	4
what	whale	whine	*The **w** is silent in these words.*
when	wheat	whisk	who
which	wheel	whisper	whose
why	whip	whistle	whom
while	whether	white	whole
where			

Answer these questions. You will need an atlas for the first five questions.

1 What is the name of the river that runs through London? ....

2 Where is Land's End? ....

3 Which cities are north of London? Southampton, Birmingham, Liverpool, Exeter,

Edinburgh. ....

N
W ← → E
S

4 The Needles lie off the coast of the Isle of Wight. What are they and why do they have

that name? ....

Copy this map →

Southampton

The Needles   The Isle of Wight

→

5	*True or false (untrue)?*	answer
	(a) Edinburgh is the capital city of Scotland.	....
	(b) Whales are often seen off the coast of Wales.	....
	(c) The city of Sheffield is in Yorkshire.	....

6 When is your birthday? ....

7 If a whole cake is cut into two equal pieces what is each piece called? ....

8 At what time of the year do farmers cut the wheat? ....

9 What colour is snow when it falls? ....

10 From whom do you buy fruit? ....

11 What is the name of the wheel we keep in the boot of the car? ....

ck

Say the ck like the k in kite.   *The vowels have a short sound.*

ack	eck	ick	ock	uck
1	**2**	**3**	**4**	**5**
back	deck	kick	dock	duck
Jack	neck	Mick	lock	luck
pack	peck	pick	rock	truck
sack	check	sick	sock	stuck
crack		brick	socket	struck
smack		trick	pocket	bucket
black		thick	clock	
slacks		ticket	frock	
jacket		chicken	shock	
packet		quick	knock	

Complete the words in the story. Choose from the words that are underlined.

THE HIJACK

The tr _ _ _ driver l _ _ _ ed the door of his tr _ _ _ . He put the keys in his

j _ _ _ et po _ _ _ _ and walked into the café . The watching men ch _ _ _ ed that he was

wearing a bl _ _ _ j _ _ _ et, bl _ _ _ sl _ _ _ _ and a white polo-n _ _ _ ed jumper.

'That's him,' said J _ _ _ . 'On time, too. With l _ _ _ we'll be home by six

o'cl _ _ _ .'

The driver was eating ch _ _ _ en and chips. J _ _ _ and M _ _ _ had the same. The

driver's coat hung over the b _ _ _ of his chair. The rest was easy.

The two men got up. As they passed by the table M _ _ _ tripped and kn _ _ _ ed

over the driver's tea. Jack qu _ _ _ ly p _ _ _ ed the keys out of his j _ _ _ et po _ _ _ _ .

They both left.

'Hold it!'

Jack and Mick froze with sh _ _ _ . They were facing seven very tall policemen. They

did not move. The tr _ _ _ driver came out. He took the keys out of Jack's po _ _ _ _

and smiled.

'Glad you didn't get str _ _ _ on the head, sergeant,' someone said.

Jack and Mick looked s _ _ _ _ . Someone had tr _ _ _ ed them and now they would get

a prison sentence.

A fair cop, some would say!

ck*

		Change the first letter of the old word to make a new word that fits the new meaning.		
	old word	meaning of new word	new word	
1	back	This is a boy's name. It is also a tool that is used to lift a car so that a wheel can be changed.	....
2	pack	This is what you get when you lose your job.	....
3	packet	This is the name of a short coat. It is part of a suit.	....
4	slack	Coal is this colour.	....
5	deck	This is the part of the body between the head and shoulders.	....
6	pick	Footballers do this to a football.	....
7	lick	If you eat something bad it may make you feel like this.	....
8	tricks	Most houses or flats are made of these.	....
9	wicket	If you travel on a train you must have one of these.	....
10	dock	A key turns in this.	....
11	sock	I am a large stone.	....
12	block	This tells the time.	....
13	pocket	An electric light bulb or a plug fits into this.	....
14	luck	This bird quacks.	....

Three-letter blends; str*

1	2	3	4
strap	streak	strict	stroke
strangle	stream	string	strong
strain	street	strip	struggle
strange	stretch	stripe	instruct
stray		stride	strength
straw		strike	straight

Complete the words with spaces in them. Choose from the words that are underlined.

1 I saw a _ _ _ _ _ ge object in the sky and my friend said it was a U.F.O. (What do these letters stand for?)

2 My father lifted something heavy at work and _ _ _ ained his back.

3 You have to put fresh _ _ _ _ w in your hamster's cage every week.

4 You have to be very _ _ _ _ ng and fit to play a good game of football.

5 'What is a stream?' I asked the Geography teacher. She said, 'A str _ _ _ , in this case, is like a river, but it is not as wide as a river.' Then she added, 'It has another meaning. Do you know what it is?' (Discuss the other meaning with your teacher.)

6 Do you think that zebras are black with white _ _ _ _ _ _ s or white with black _ _ _ _ _ _ s?

7 We never let our cat go out in the _ _ _ eet in case she crosses the road and gets run over.

8 Last week I had flu. I was so ill that I didn't have the _ _ _ _ _ _ th to get up for three days.

9 The ships were _ _ _ _ tched out in a straig _ _ line as far as the eye could see.

10 The P.E. teacher says he will inst _ _ _ _ us in the art of Judo when we are in the fourth year.

11 Our Maths teacher is very str _ _ _ .

12 My mother said we had to go without our sweets because Dad is on _ _ _ _ ke.

Three-letter blends; str*

Complete the words in the story.

Choose from these words:

struggle	straight	stray	strength	street	stroked
streaks	strange	stripe	stretched	stronger	straighten
string	strict	strangle	struck	strap	strips

BLACKY

Last week I found a _ _ _ ay kitten mewing in the _ _ _ _ _ t outside our flats.
I picked him up and he tried to str _ _ _ _ _ free but he didn't have the stren _ _ _ , poor
thing.

I stro _ _ _ him gently and after a while he stret _ _ _ _ out in my arms and started
to purr. I looked at him closely. He was thin and his black fur was matted and dirty. A
white str _ _ _ ran strai _ _ _ along his back and there were tiny stre _ _ _ of white on
his legs. He was a stran _ _ little kitten but I wanted to keep him.

I have always wanted a cat and the rules about pets aren't so stri _ _ in our flats now.
I took him upstairs as I felt sure I would be able to keep him.

When Mum opened the door I thrust the kitten into her arms . 'Poor little thing,' I said.
'I found him outside in the cold.' When I looked at Mum's face I didn't have to ask if I
could keep him. My mother loves cats too.

After we had fed Blacky, as we named him, he seemed much str _ _ _ _ _ '. So we found
some stri _ _ and started to play with him but he got tangled up in the string.

'Be careful he doesn't stran _ _ _ himself,' Mum said as I str _ _ ghtened out the
str _ _ _ .

Next I rolled some silver paper into a ball. Blacky str _ ck the ball everytime I threw
it to him but he soon tired of that game so I picked him up.

He started to nibble my watch str _ _ and my gold chain. Then he struggled to get
down. He began to sharpen his claws on the morning paper and tore it into tiny str _ ps.
He played until he was tired out and by the time Dad got in he was stre _ _ _ _ _ out on
the floor fast asleep.

Even Dad had to admit that Blacky was a welcome new member of our family.

Three-letter blends; scr, spr, spl*

scr		spr	spl
1 scramble scrap scrape scratch scream screech	**2** screen script scrub screw describe	**3** sprain sprang spray spring sprinkle sprite spread	**4** splash splendid splinter split splutter

Complete the words in the story. Choose from the words that are underlined.

THE CHASE

The spr _ _ from the motor-boat fanned out in the wind. Moon scr _ _ med at Angie to sit down seconds before a shot whistled through the air and smashed into the winds _ _ _ _ _ . Spl _ _ _ ers of the scr _ _ _ flew everywhere, one making a deep scr _ _ _ _ across Moon's cheek.

'OK?' he asked.

'OK.' She smiled and scr _ _ _ led over the seats to join him by the wheel.

He opened the throttle wider and the Sea Witch spr _ _ g forward. They were gaining on the Sea Spr _ t _ now and Moon could clearly see Mr Springer at the wheel with Tate by his side.

Tate raised his arm at the same moment as Moon heard the Sea Witch's engine spl _ _ _ _ _ and die. Angie fell back as the boat rocked helplessly in the wake of the Sea Spr _ _ _ , which was now just a dot in the distance.

'Well,' Moon thought, 'their day will come.' He turned to Angie. She tried to smile. 'Just a spr _ _ _ , not a bullet,' she explained. 'Sorry. I'm not much help, am I?'

Moon found a blanket and spr _ _ _ it over her. 'We're in a fix now, aren't we?' she said. 'We haven't a scr _ _ to eat and only a little water.'

Moon patted her arm. 'We'll manage,' he said. 'Something will turn up.'

Why are Moon and Angie chasing Mr Springer and Tate?

1   *Make up a story with* The Chase *as the middle part. Add a good ending. Each person must tell part of the story.*

2   *Draw a picture of the story.*

scr, spr, spl crossword*

Choose from these words:

scramble   scrape   screw

scratch   scream   screen

describe   sprain   spring

spray   splash   split

Clues across

1   I saw the bank robber and the policeman asked me to _ _ _ _ _ _ _ _ him.

5   The first season of the year is _ _ _ _ _ _ .

7   I was fishing from the rocks when the tide came in and I had to _ _ _ _ _ _ _ _ back over the rocks to get to the beach.

8   We saw a film on the small _ _ _ _ _ _ in Studio 1.

11   My shoes were caked with mud when I came in and my mother made me _ _ _ _ _ _ the mud off them.

12   I fell over and the seam of my skirt _ _ _ _ _ open.

Clues down

2   I was playing with my cat when she gave me a bad _ _ _ _ _ _ _ on my cheek.

3   I limped into the classroom and the teacher said, 'How did you _ _ _ _ _ _ your ankle?'

4   John fell into the swimming pool with a big _ _ _ _ _ _ .

6   My sister locked me in the shed and I was so scared that I started to _ _ _ _ _ _ .

9   I need one more _ _ _ _ _ to finish the table I'm making.

10   As the boat sped over the waves the _ _ _ _ _ splashed our faces.

thr and shr*

thr			shr	
1	**2**	**3**	**4**	**5**
three	throw	thread	shriek	shred
throat	threw	threat	shrug	shrimp
throne	thrush	threaten	shrub	shrink
throb	thrust	through	shrill	shrivel
thrill	thrash	throttle		

What am I?	
clues	answers
1 I am the front part of the neck.	
2 I am ten minus seven.	
3 I have many meanings. One of them is from end to end: I walked _ _ _ _ _ _ _ the park.	
4 I mean to make threats.	
5 I am a garden bird with a speckled breast.	
6 I am a raised chair for a King or Queen.	
7 I am the past tense of the word throw.	
8 I am another name for the cotton or nylon you use for sewing. I also mean to pass the cotton through the eye of a needle.	
9 I mean to push with force.	
10 I am a small shell-fish.	
11 I am another name for a scream.	
12 I mean a scrap of something. I also mean to cut or tear into small pieces.	
13 I mean to become smaller.	
14 I am a small bush.	
15 I mean to raise the shoulders.	

G1

o saying ŭ

Say the o like the u in cup. Learn how to spell these words.

son	come	cover	month	London
won	some	discover	money	wonder
ton	something	other	honey	worry
done	nothing	another	Monday	comfort
none	love	mother	oven	compass
does	glove	brother	dozen	among
	above		front	tongue

Choose from the words that are underlined.

Clues across

1 In 1492 Columbus sailed across the Atlantic to try to
_ _ _ _ _ _ _ _ India.

5 My mother bakes cakes in the _ _ _ _ .

7 I came first in the running race and _ _ _ a medal.

8 I feel sick if I sit in the back seat of the car so I always sit in the _ _ _ _ _ seat.

10 Every time I buy sweets my little sister wants _ _ _ _ _ of them.

12 I did not know the time and I said to my friend,
'I _ _ _ _ _ _ what the time is.'

14 Bees are always busy making _ _ _ _ _ .

15 I would like to go to France for a holiday but it costs too much _ _ _ _ _ _ .

16 The shop assistant asked, 'Would you like to try on this dress first?'
'No, I'll try the _ _ _ _ _ one first,' I replied.

Clues down

1 Where _ _ _ _ your mother work?' asked the teacher.
2 My mother told me to _ _ _ _ _ the meat with a plate because of the flies.
3 My sister is pleased she had a baby boy last week because she had always wanted a _ _ _ .
4 If you look at a map of Britain you will see that Scotland is _ _ _ _ _ England.
6 When I went to buy another compass there were _ _ _ _ left.
9 My brother is in hospital but my father told me not to _ _ _ _ _ because he is better.
11 May is the fifth _ _ _ _ _ of the year.
13 My teacher was angry when I said that I had not _ _ _ _ my homework.

Compound words

All these words have 2 parts which are called syllables.

A *Join a word in column 1 to a word in column 2 and make a new word.*

short vowels		long vowels	
1	**2**	**1**	**2**
hand _ _ _	man	life _ _ _ _	bow
milk _ _ _	set	sea _ _ _ _	maid
sun _ _ _	cuffs	bee _ _ _ _	line
pad _ _ _ _	pet	pipe _ _ _ _	boat
wind _ _ _ _	mill	rain _ _ _ _	weed
up _ _ _	lock	rain _ _ _	hive
hand _ _ _ _ _	bag	brides _ _ _ _	coat
him _ _ _ _	self	rail _ _ _	table
pup _ _ _	set	time _ _ _ _ _	way

B *Complete each word.*

Choose from these words:

come	times	bone	board
ball	get	after	snow

1 The spine is some _ _ _ _ _ called the back _ _ _ _ .

2 Our class won the foot _ _ _ _ match.

3 Our games lesson is in the _ _ _ _ _ noon and we must not for _ _ _ our kit.

4 When it snows a lot you can throw snowballs and make a _ _ _ _ man.

5 The teacher always locks our books in the cup _ _ _ _ _ before she goes home.

6 You will be _ _ _ _ very fat if you eat too many cakes and sweets.

Syllables*

A syllable is a group of letters said together which make a part of a word.

1-syllable words	2-syllable words	3-syllable words
hand	window	newspaper
kite	parrot	elephant
hills	teapot	butterfly
ring	pencil	telephone
tree	arrow	violin
sun	toothbrush	seventeen
tie	padlock	umbrella
snake	snowman	camera
moon	armchair	bicycle
cup	zebra	banana

Vowel y: some examples

y saying ē			y saying ī	y saying ĭ
many	sunny	twenty	apply	syrup
heavy	windy	empty	supply	system
ready	angry	lady	reply	syllable
hurry	hungry	baby	multiply	pyramid
carry	happy	tiny	try	oxygen
sorry	lazy	nobody	type	
pretty	family	company	tyre	sympathy
				mystery

Choose from the words that are underlined.

Clues across

1 I could not carry the suitcase because it was too _ _ _ _ _ .

4 My family went out early but I didn't go with them because I was not _ _ _ _ _ in time.

5 I sent a letter to Bristol to apply for a job but I didn't get a _ _ _ _ _ .

6 'I can't multiply 58 by 9.' 'That's because you don't _ _ _ ,' said Dad.

10 'How _ _ _ _ people can type already?' asked the teacher.

11 My girlfriend has long blonde hair and is very _ _ _ _ _ _ .

12 We had a puncture because a tiny nail had stuck in the _ _ _ _ _ .

13 It was a sunny day but nobody was on the beach because it was very _ _ _ _ _ _ .

Clues down

1 My friend said we would be late for the film if we didn't _ _ _ _ _ _ .

2 I am going to _ _ _ _ _ for a job with the British Oxygen Company.

3 My cat sleeps all day because she is very _ _ _ _ _ .

7 I like to read a good _ _ _ _ _ _ _ story.

8 I wanted some syrup on my toast but I couldn't have any because the tin was _ _ _ _ _ .

9 When I tread on someone's toe I say _ _ _ _ _ _ .

Days of the week

Sunday	Monday	Tuesday	Wednesday	Thursday	Friday	Saturday

1 .... is the first day of the week.

2 Monday comes before ....

3 .... and Sunday are the weekend days.

4 Sunday comes before ....

5 Wednesday is in the middle of the week. Wednesday comes before ....

6 Saturday comes after ....

7 Thursday comes after ....

Months of the year

January	February	March	April	May	June
July	August	September	October	November	December

This is one way of writing a date of birth: (a) <u>4.3.66</u> ....

When you put the month in writing it becomes: (b) <u>4th March 1966</u> ....

1 Now write your date of birth in these two different ways: (a) ....

  (b) ....

We put **th** *after every number except 1, 2 and 3 where*
we have 1st, 2nd and 3rd (21st, 22nd, 23rd).

2 What is the 5th month of the year? ....

3 What is the 11th month of the year? ....

4 Which month comes before October? ....

5 During which months is the weather very cold? ....

....

6 In which month does Christmas Day fall? ....

7 Which month comes after December and before February? ....

8 Which month comes before March? ....

9 Which month comes after July? ....

Colours*

Colour in the pattern then learn how to spell the words.

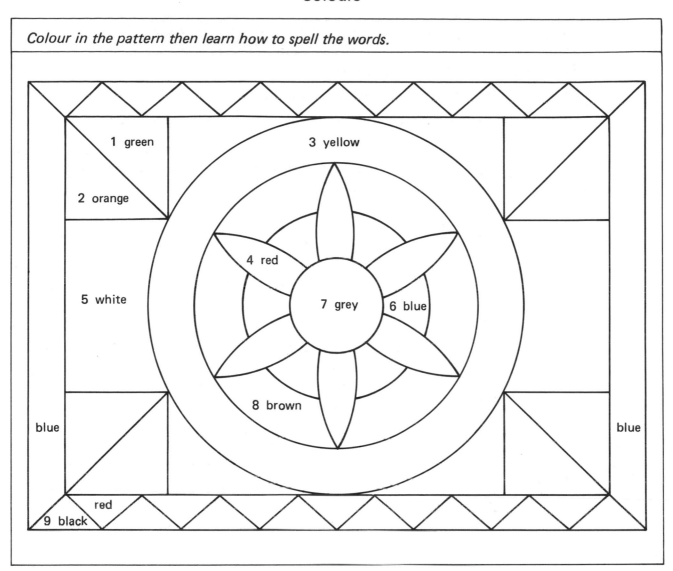

1 green
2 orange
3 yellow
4 red
5 white
6 blue
7 grey
8 brown
9 black
blue
blue
red

Write the colours here:

1   2   3   4   5

6   7   8   9

The pattern above is made up of these shapes:

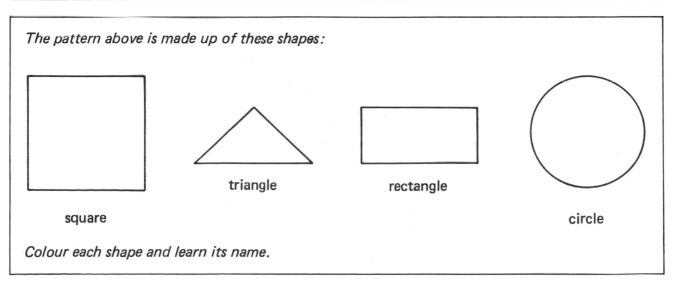

square   triangle   rectangle   circle

Colour each shape and learn its name.

ain*

Say the **ain** like the **ain** in **rain**.

Cut along the dotted lines between the triangles.

Cut off the strip of paper containing **ain** and slide it through the slots.

Starting at the top with **g**, move the paper down so that the **ain** is beside each letter in turn.

1	g
2	m
3	p
4	r
5	br
6	dr
7	gr
8	tr
9	pl
10	Sp
11	st
12	str
13	spr
14	ch
15	obt
16	rem
17	cont
18	expl

ain

Complete the words with spaces. Choose from the words on the left.

1   The sky is very black. Do you think it is going to r _ _ _ ?

2   You have to use your b _ _ _ _ when you do your lessons.

3   I had a bad p _ _ _ in my ankle and the teacher said, 'I think you have s _ _ _ _ _ ed it.'

4   I went to the post office to o _ _ _ _ _ _ a stamp for my letter to S _ _ _ _ _ .

5   The t _ _ _ _ for Leeds leaves from King's Cross m _ _ _ line station.

6   I washed my jeans when I spilt ink on them, but it still left a s _ _ _ _ _ .

7   My biggest Christmas present was wrapped in p _ _ _ _ paper. 'What does it c _ _ _ _ _ _ _ ?' I asked.

8   It was raining and I had to r _ _ _ _ _ _ inside because I had a cold.

9   Our road was flooded the other day because a d _ _ _ _ _ was blocked.

10   My sister gave me a gold cross and c _ _ _ _ _ for my birthday.

11   Don't read in poor light because you will s _ _ _ _ _ _ your eyes.

12   I asked the teacher to e _ _ _ _ _ _ _ the History homework.

all and alk crossword

Learn how to spell all these words.

Choose from these words:

all	ball
call	hall
tall	walls
small	stall
fall	talk
walk	

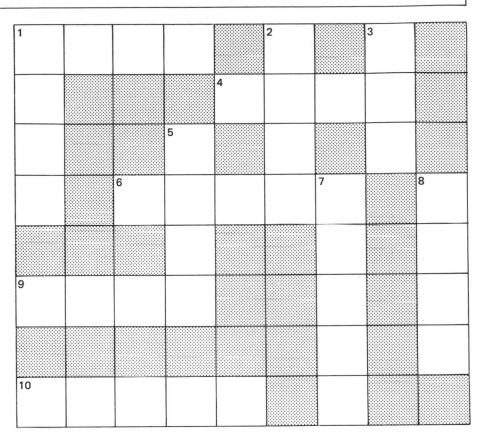

Clues across

1 My friend said, 'My height is five feet. How _ _ _ _ are you?'

4 Sue said, 'If I go to the club tonight I'll come and _ _ _ _ for you.'

6 We stuck our paintings on two _ _ _ _ _ of the classroom.

9 The foot _ _ _ _ hit the goal-post and we all groaned.

10 Every Saturday I work on a fruit _ _ _ _ _ in the market.

Clues down

1 The teacher told us that we must not _ _ _ _ during the exam.

2 When my little sister asked me if she could have a ride on my bike I said, 'Yes, but don't _ _ _ _ off.'

3 We have had three cats and _ _ _ of them have been called Lucy.

5 As our shoes were very muddy Dad told us to take them off and leave them in the _ _ _ _ .

7 I wanted a blue jacket in a large size but the shop only had _ _ _ _ _ sizes left.

8 I take my dog for a _ _ _ _ every morning and evening.

ight (ite)*

Say the ight like the ite in kite.

Cut along the dotted lines between the triangles.

Cut off the strip of paper containing ight and slide it through the slots.

Starting at the top with f, move the paper down so that the ight is beside each letter in turn.

1	f
2	l
3	m
4	n
5	r
6	s
7	t
8	fl
9	he
10	br
11	fr
12	sl

ight

Complete the words with spaces.
Choose from the words on the left.

THE FIGHT

Our cat went out last n _ _ _ _ and had a

f _ _ _ _ with the big ginger tom-cat next door.

He was in full f _ _ _ _ _ over the high

garden fence as we opened the back door, and when

he rushed in he seemed very f _ _ _ _ _ ened.

My little brother picked him up. In the

l _ _ _ _ we saw that he had a sl _ _ _ _ _ cut

above his r _ _ _ _ eye.

'He m _ _ _ _ have lost his s _ _ _ _ _ ,

sobbed my sister. 'Poor little Smokey.'

'His lovely br _ _ _ _ eyes are so sad,' cried

my brother as he clung t _ _ _ _ ly to the

fr _ _ _ _ ened cat.

My mother sighed. 'He's such a small cat but

he's brave for his h _ _ _ _ _ ,' she said.

She picked up the brave bundle of fur and

bathed the cut above his r _ _ _ _ eye.

As she stroked him he began to purr and we

knew that he had already forgotten his f _ _ _ _

with the ginger cat next door.

The suffix ing*

A suffix is a letter, or group of letters (syllable), which is placed at the end of a <u>root</u> word to change its meaning and make a new word. Example: **tell** (root word) + **ing** (suffix) = **telling**.

A   Read the root words. Add **ing** *to each word. Read the new words.*

1		2		3	
go	.........going.........	cry	....	see	....
meet	....	try	....	say	....
feel	....	play	....	jump	....
rain	....	think	....	look	....

These words are easy to spell because you just add **ing** *to the root word.*

B   Before you add **ing** *to these words you must leave out the* **e**.

1		2		3	
come	......coming......	use	....	smile	....
make	....	move	....	drive	....
have	....	wave	....	dance	....
take	....	save	....	leave	....

C   Before you add **ing** *to these words you must double the last letter.*

1		2		3	
sit	......sitting......	tap	....	grin	....
hit	....	stop	....	slip	....
run	....	clap	....	swim	....
get	....	shop	....	travel	....

Now learn how to spell all the **ing** *words in B and C.*

D   Write a sentence about each of these: (1) A swimming pool
(2) Mum or Dad out shopping   (3) A boat or plane travelling to another country.

....

....

....

....

....

....

The suffix **ed** (1)*

The suffix **ed** has three sounds: **d, t** and **ĭd**.

A Add **ed** to the following root words.

ed saying **d**		ed saying **t**		ed saying **ĭd** — after root words ending in **d** or **t**	
1		**2**		**3**	
open	....	help	....	start	....
play	....	lock	....	shout	....
call	....	check	....	lift	....
fill	....	pick	....	wait	....
rain	....	look	....	want	....
cover	....	walk	....	point	....
seem	....	mix	....	add	....
happen	....	ask	....	land	....
snow	....	finish	....	heat	....

B Complete each sentence by putting the words at the side in the right order.

The thief .... house. He looked around him and checked that nobody was there.

　He .... the door and went in. He seemed very confident. He helped himself to a biscuit from a jar and .... of gin and tonic.

　He .... then he started to ransack the dining room. He lifted two silver cups into his bag .... of a small box.

　He checked each bedroom. He knew exactly what he wanted. The contents of another box .... bag.

　When he had finished he went to the telephone .... 'I shall be late home. I have some work to do at the office.'

　'All right, dear. Will you be home .... 'We'll eat about eight.'

　'Yes,' he replied and put the phone down. He looked around him once more then left. He .... and walked away. .... in ten minutes.

up the	
walked to	
opened the	
picked lock,	
a mixed	
himself drink	
two minutes	
for waited	
and contents	
the added	
tipped his	
were into	
his called	
wife. and	
she dinner?'	
asked. for	
door front	
the closed	
all happened	
had It	

The suffix ed (2)*

In words ending in e leave off the e and add ed. Or you can remember it this way: words ending in e simply add d.	In these words double the last letter before you add ed.	In these words change the y to i before you add ed.
1	**2**	**3**
scare .... scared	stop .... stopped	cry .... cried
stroke	shop	try ....
arrive	slip	fry ....
rescue	tap	dry ....
scramble	clap	reply ....
struggle	trap	apply ....
move	trip	hurry ....
escape	nod	marry ....
	pat	worry ....
	skid	carry ....
	grin	
	grab	

Selton Journal

15p

Wednesday 12th April 19 . . . .

Page 1

CHILDREN STILL MISSING

by Alan Waters

Ann and Peter Reeves

Yesterday another rescue party was sent out into dense Selton Forest to find Ann and Peter Reeves, the two children who have been missing since Friday night.

They found the following strange story (printed on page 3) written on a torn piece of paper which had been left in an old hut near the centre of the forest.

Anyone who can throw any light on the disappearance of these two children is asked to ring the local police on 052 11735.

continued on page I4

The suffix **ed** (2)

continued from page I3

Before you can read what is written on the piece of paper you have to complete the words with spaces.

Choose from these words:

moved	rescued	stopped	seemed	tripped	patted	scrambled
struggled	scared	nodded	trapped	grinned	worried	pointed
cried	happened	escaped	started	replied	hurried	arrived

Selton Journal

LETTER FROM THE MISSING CHILDREN

continued from page 1

Last Friday we lost our way in the forest. I felt very sc _ _ _ _ and Ann cr _ _ _ for a long time. I p _ _ _ _ _ her arm to try to comfort her and at last she st _ _ _ _ _ .

'Mum will be w _ _ _ _ _ _ if we haven't ar _ _ _ _ _ home by nine o'clock,' she said. I n _ _ _ _ _ and re _ _ _ _ _ _ ,

'We'll soon find the way out.'

We scr _ _ _ _ _ _ up a steep bank and h _ _ _ _ _ _ down a small path which see _ _ _ to lead away from the dense part of the forest. Ann suddenly tri _ _ _ _ over a hidden tree stump and

Page 3

sank into the undergrowth. I gave her my hand and she str _ _ _ _ _ _ to stand up.

We stood there in the silence. Darkness had fallen quickly and Ann knew as well as I did that we were now tr _ _ _ _ _ . She st _ _ _ _ _ to cry again. 'Do you think we'll be res _ _ _ _ before morning?'

'Maybe,' I said. I was looking into the darkness. A pinpoint of light seemed to be getting closer. 'In fact I'm sure we will.' I gr _ _ _ _ _ as I saw the light dancing between the trees and point _ _ towards it. 'There!'

Ann saw the light and m _ _ _ _ quickly away from me towards it. What h _ _ _ _ _ _ _ next is difficult for me to tell except that I think it is now Monday and we have not es _ _ _ _ _ from the horrors of the forest. Will we be left to die here?

What did happen when Ann ran towards the light? What was the light?
Why are they still trapped in the forest?

Do one of the following:

1 *Each person <u>tell</u> a part of the ending of the story.*

2 *<u>Write</u> the ending of the story.*

3 *Make up a <u>play</u> based on this story. Add your own ending.*

The suffix ly (lēe)

A Add **ly** to the root word.			
1	**2**	**3** Before you add **ly** to these two-syllable words ending in **y**, change the **y** to **i**	**4** When you see words of more than one syllable that end in **le**, change the **e** to **y**.
careful ..carefully....	exact		
quick	silent		
quiet	sad		
tight	neat	happy ...happily....	sensible ...sensibly....
slow	sudden	lucky	horrible ....
love	soft	easy	reasonable...................
hopeful	loud	sleepy	irritable ....

B Complete each sentence by putting the words at the side in the right order.

1 The pupils were very noisy and the teacher wanted them to be silent.

'Be quiet,' she said. 'Do your work ....

.... stay behind after school.'

| or | silently |
| will | you |

2 I am very slow at getting ready in the morning. My mother said, 'If you

dress this ....

be late for school.'

| will | always |
| slowly | you |

3 You must always have the exact fare ready when you get on our buses.

The driver always shouts, 'Have ....

.... please', as we get on.

| exactly | right |
| money | the |

4 My sister's baby is such a happy little boy. He never cries and plays

.... all day.

| with | happily |
| his | toys |

5 I .... biology drawings.

The teacher gave me A and wrote underneath, 'Neat, careful work.'

| labelled | all |
| carefully | my |

6 Our teacher thinks we aren't very sensible people. When we go to a

museum he always says, 'Now, ...

.... in the museum.'

| must | behave |
| sensibly | you |

7 Our dog had a sudden fit and died. 'Never mind,' Mum said, ...

.... she didn't suffer.'

| 'as | died |
| suddenly | she |

Contractions (1)*

A contraction is usually one word standing for two words.
One or more letters are left out and we put in an apostrophe instead, as in don't (do not).

A These contractions are used a lot in everyday speech.
   Write the two words each contraction represents.

n't = not		's = is	're = are
isn't .....is.... ...not...	couldn't	he's	you're ....
wasn't	wouldn't	she's	we're ....
aren't	shouldn't	it's	they're ....
haven't		there's	**'m = am**
hasn't	can't ......cannot	that's	I'm ....
hadn't	shan't .....shall... not..	here's	
don't	won't .....will... not..	what's	**'s = us**
doesn't		where's	
didn't		who's	let's ....

B Answer these questions by putting the right words from the box in the spaces.

	Is it a sunny day? No, it .... a sunny day, ... raining.	it's isn't
	Are these people happy? No they .... happy, ... sad.	aren't they're
	Can you buy this boat? No, you .... because .... sold.	it's can't

C Complete these sentences.

1 I can't ....

2 I'm ....

3 You're ....

Contractions   (2)

Write the words each contraction represents.

've = have	'll = will	'd = would or had
I've	I'll	I'd *I* *would* , *I* *had*
you've	you'll	you'd .... , ...
we've	she'll	he'd .... , ...
they've	he'll	she'd .... , ...
	we'll	we'd .... , ...
	they'll	they'd .... , ...

This play contains many contractions.

SATURDAY AFTERNOON

Scene 1   The Barnett family's dining room. The time is 2pm.

Dad: As we've nothing to do this afternoon let's go window shopping for a new car.

Pat: What's window shopping?

Dad: It's when you look at all the things displayed in the shop window, without buying anything.

Mum: It's about time we really looked for a new car, isn't it?
It won't be long before our car falls to pieces.

John: You can say that again. It won't run for much longer unless you spend some money on it.

Dad: I might have to do that. Anyway, who's for a trip around the showrooms?

Mum: Fine with me.

Pat: They've got some good second-hand cars in Hill Motors, Dad.

John: Isn't that where our Mini came from?

Dad: Yes, that's a good idea. We'll go there first.

(They visit Hill motors and five other showrooms. Finally they come to Hunt Motors.)

Scene 2   Inside Hunt Motors' showroom.

Dad: Now that's a good car. (He points to a blue Cortina.)

Pat: We can't afford that, Dad.

Dad: No you're right, but I'd like a big car.

Mum: I prefer small cars.

continued on page 18

Contractions   (2)

continued from page 17

Dad: Well, at least you're easy to please.

(John is looking inside a small car near the window.)

John: Let's have a Fiat like this one, Dad. They have a good name, don't they?

Dad: Yes, but I'd like an English car.

Mum: As we all seem to have different ideas about the best car to buy we'll have to make do with our old car.

Pat: Come on, then. I'm getting tired of looking at cars.

(They leave the showroom, get into their car and start for home.)

Scene 3   In the car.

Mum: I can smell smoke.

Dad: Can you? I can't.

Mum: Aren't you going to stop the car?

Pat: I can smell it too. Stop the car, Dad.

(Dad stops the car and everyone gets out. Smoke is now pouring out of the engine.

John lifts up the bonnet.)

John: It looks like an oil leak. We can't drive home in case it catches fire.

Pat: You'll have to get rid of this car, Dad. It's a heap of junk now.

Dad (angrily):   We've had good use out of this car for the past eight years.

Mum: You're right, dear. It's never let us down.

Pat: Sorry, Dad, but what are we going to do? I'm meeting Linda at 6.30.

John: We can ring the AA. As we haven't broken down outside our own house they'll come and look at the car.

Mum: Do you think it will have to be towed away?

John: I don't know but I'll ask the people in that house if I can use their phone.

(He knocks on the door and goes inside.)

Mum: Oh dear, what a way for a lovely Saturday afternoon to end.

Make up a short play of your own called The Breakdown.

o͞o (1)

The first sound of **oo** is like the **oo** in **moon**.				
1	**2**	**3**	**4**	**5**
moon	food	cool	zoo	hoop
soon	mood	fool	roof	loop
noon	boot	pool	hoof	stoop
afternoon	hoot	spool	proof	troop
spoon	root	tool	choose	**harder words**
broom	shoot	stool	ooze	harpoon
gloomy	tooth	school	loose	monsoon
zoom	smooth	too	goose	typhoon

A Change the <u>first</u> letter of the old word to make a new word that fits the new meaning.

old word		new meaning	new word
1	fool	Not too hot.	....
2	pool	We use this to make things.	....
3	mood	We eat this to live.	....
4	goose	Not tight.	....
5	boots	Plants grow these underground.	....
6	soon	This shines at night.	....
7	too	You can see many different wild animals in this place.	....

B Change the <u>last</u> letter of the old word to make a new word that fits the new meaning.

1	stoop	You can sit on this. It has three legs.	....
2	hoop	Owls make this noise.	....
3	room	This is on the top of the house.	....
4	spool	We eat our soup with this.	....

ŏŏ (2)

The second sound of oo is like the oo in book.			The oo in these words has a different sound.	
1	**2**	**3**	**4**	**5**
book	crook	<u>foot</u>	<u>blood</u>	<u>door</u>
<u>cook</u>	crooked	soot	<u>flood</u>	floor
hook	<u>good</u>	wool	brooch	<u>poor</u>
<u>look</u>	hood			moor
<u>took</u>	<u>wood</u>			
<u>shook</u>	<u>stood</u>			

Complete the words with spaces. Choose from the words that are underlined.

IN A VICTORIAN KITCHEN

I was dreaming of the party we were going to have on Queen Victoria's wedding day when the plate of meat I was holding slipped out of my hands.

The c _ _ _ just st _ _ _ there and I _ _ ked at me. Then she reached out, t _ _ _ me by the arms and sh _ _ _ me for what seemed like five minutes. Without a word she left the kitchen; the d _ _ _ slammed and I broke into a fl _ _ _ of tears.

After a while I stopped crying but I was still feeling very gloomy when Alice came in with w _ _ _ for the fire.

'What's all this on the fl _ _ r, Jane?' she asked as she bent down to pick up a piece of the plate. 'Now, dry your eyes and pick these up. Mrs Field is not going to be very pleased; this is her g _ _ _ dinner set.' She pushed the pieces with her f _ _ t. 'Don't bother to explain, just clean the fl _ _ _ .'

Slowly I picked up the pieces of plate and meat. A splinter of china pricked my finger and drops of bl _ _ _ dripped onto my apron. 'Mrs Field won't like that either,' I said to myself. 'One day I'll leave this kitchen and not come back.' But I knew this wasn't true. I was doomed to be a p _ _ _ kitchen maid for the rest of my life; this was going to be my home for ever.

Discuss with your teacher what life was like for poor people in Victorian England (1837 – 1901).

oo crossword

Choose from these words:

tooth	cool	pool
cook	hood	door
zoo	shoot	spoon
tool	took	blood
soon	afternoon	moon

Clues across

1   In the desert the evening air is not hot; it is very _ _ _ _ .

2   We go swimming in a swimming _ _ _ _ .

5   You must always clean your teeth with a good _ _ _ _ _ brush.

7   The _ _ _ _ shines in the sky at night.

9   Never open the oven _ _ _ _ while a cake is cooking.

11   The _ _ _ _ _ carries oxygen to all parts of the body.

12   Last week I _ _ _ _ my sister to see 'Moonraker' at the Odeon.

13   I use a small _ _ _ _ _ to eat my cornflakes.

Clues down

1   I like our school dinners. We have a very good _ _ _ _ _ .

3   When my mother asked me to dry the dishes I said, 'I'll do them as _ _ _ _ as I've finished my homework.'

4   The time between noon (12 o'clock midday) and the evening is called the _ _ _ _ _ _ _ _ _ .

5   My father keeps his tools in a big wooden _ _ _ _ box.

6   My woollen coat has a _ _ _ _ which keeps my head warm in winter.

8   The bank robber said, 'Stand still or I'll _ _ _ _ _ !'

10   We can see wild animals in the _ _ _ .

er*

When **er** comes at the end of a word of more than one syllable,
it has the sound of the **er** in **butter**.

1	2	3	4
<u>butter</u>	<u>enter</u>	poster	spider
better	<u>number</u>	<u>remember</u>	<u>summer</u>
<u>letter</u>	offer	slipper	together
litter	<u>water</u>	<u>shiver</u>	<u>temper</u>
clever	<u>paper</u>	shelter	<u>under</u>
<u>danger</u>	passenger	finger	thunder

A In the word search below find all the words that are underlined.
Draw a ring around each word.

t	x	m	n	o	v	r	f	v	z	s	h	i	v	e	r	d
e	l	m	p	z	e	e	q	t	s	f	q	z	m	z	n	z
m	z	s	l	d	q	m	f	l	d	a	n	g	e	r	x	l
p	k	j	n	f	v	e	w	p	r	n	b	k	j	v	r	m
e	j	u	x	n	u	m	b	e	r	m	j	u	p	e	s	n
r	t	r	z	s	s	b	s	f	p	x	r	q	t	d	d	o
w	v	p	v	y	p	e	x	s	q	j	q	t	w	t	z	p
v	l	c	a	f	p	r	n	j	l	f	e	z	a	k	e	q
y	n	o	a	p	x	v	l	t	x	l	q	j	t	z	j	r
m	x	z	d	x	e	j	x	y	e	c	z	s	e	l	v	z
s	u	m	m	e	r	r	z	r	e	r	d	c	r	o	q	x

Learn how to spell these words.

B Put each word in a sentence:
(1) clever (2) passenger (3) better (4) thunder (5) remember.

....

....

....

....

....

er, ir, ur

In these words **er**, **ir** and **ur** sound like the **ur** in **church**.

er	ir	ur
1	**2**	**3**
kerb	girl	<u>turn</u>
herd	<u>first</u>	<u>burn</u>
nerve	thirsty	<u>hurt</u>
<u>serve</u>	<u>dirty</u>	<u>nurse</u>
<u>swerve</u>	shirt	<u>surname</u>
stern	<u>skirt</u>	<u>surgery</u>
<u>term</u>	<u>stir</u>	murder
<u>person</u>	thirteen	curtain

Put the right word in the space. Choose from the words that are underlined.

er

1 I hope I remember that the summer _ _ _ _ begins on 28th April.

2 My uncle is a very stern _ _ _ _ _ _ and he has a bad temper.

3 The women who _ _ _ _ _ in the sweet shop make us put our sweet and ice-cream papers in the litter bin.

4 A dog ran into the road and I had to _ _ _ _ _ _ to miss it.

ir

1 I must have a drink of water because I am _ _ _ _ _ _ _ .

2 My mother said I was not to get my new _ _ _ _ _   _ _ _ _ _ .

3 When you cook spaghetti you must remember to _ _ _ _ it so that it doesn't stick together.

4 My friend came _ _ _ _ _ in the winter exams.

ur

1 I _ _ _ _ my foot yesterday.

2 Your _ _ _ _ _ _ _ is your family name.

3 I waited in the doctor's _ _ _ _ _ _ _ for over twenty minutes until it was my _ _ _ _ .

4 The school _ _ _ _ _ put some cold water on the _ _ _ _ on my hand.

ew (ū and ōō)

There is very little difference between these two sounds.

Say the **ew** *like the* **ū** *in* **cube.**			*Say the* **ew** *like* **ōō** *in* **moon.**	
1	**2**	**3**	**4**	**5**
few	ewe	news	crew	chew
new	stew	newspaper	drew	threw
renew	steward	view	grew	screw
dew	knew	skewer	brew	sewer
mew	newt	mildew	brewery	jewel
			blew	jewellery
			flew	Andrew

Choose from these words:

stew	screws	renew
ewe	flew	new
few	crew	grew
view	chew	threw

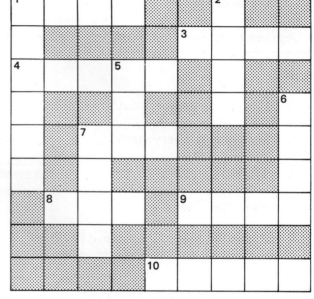

Clues across

1 We are having _ _ _ _ for dinner.

3 The ship had a _ _ _ _ of thirty men.

4 Dad said he had to _ _ _ _ _

his driving licence.

7 I need a _ _ _ boys to help me carry these books.

8 I lost my pen and my sister gave me a _ _ _ one.

9 My dog likes to _ _ _ _ a bone.

10 I _ _ _ _ _ the ball to my friend.

Clues down

1 He joined the two pieces of wood with six _ _ _ _ _ _ _ .

2 My mother _ _ _ _ some lovely flowers this summer.

5 The _ _ _ had three lambs this spring.

6 Our flat has a good _ _ _ _ of the sea.

7 My budgie _ _ _ _ away yesterday.

ew

A   Complete the words in the story.

Choose from these words:

drew	few	blew(2)	grew	knew	threw	renewed	chewed
view	crew(2)	jewels	brew	news	flew	newspapers	

THE STORM

The yacht's c _ _ _ th _ _ _ the anchor into the water. The wind bl _ _ strongly but the anchor held fast. A f _ _ of the men k _ _ _ that if the wind gr _ _ any stronger the anchor would not hold and the little boat would be tossed onto the rocks.

The black clouds f _ _ _ across the sky and what had been a clear v _ _ _ of the cliffs was now a blur of rain. Andrew ch _ _ _ _ a sweet to take his mind off the rocks, but the wind bl _ _ with r _ _ _ _ _ _ _ strength and he felt that the n _ _ _ of their shipwreck would be headlines in the next day's n _ _ _ _ _ _ _ _ _ _ .

After five hours of high seas the rain and wind died down and the sun came out. The raindrops on the deck gleamed like thousands of j _ _ _ and Andrew realised that the storm was over. He d _ _ his coat tighter to him and shivered. Time to br _ _ up a nice cup of tea, he thought.

He carefully made his way down into the cabin. His mind was at rest because he k _ _ _ that he had a very good c _ _ _ .

B   Put each word in a sentence: (1) few   (2) grew   (3) news   (4) blew   (5) jewels.

....

....

....

....

....

....

....

ture*

Say the **ture** *like the* **ture** *in* **picture.**			
1	**2**	**3**	**4**
adventure	picture	furniture	manufacture
creature	mixture	puncture	miniature
capture	fixture	signature	temperature
future	lecture	torture	departure
nature	fracture	moisture	feature

What is the word? All the words are in the columns above.	
clues	answers
1 This is the name for an exciting experience.	....
2 This word means the time to come.	....
3 This is a hole in your car tyre.	....
4 This is one word which means the things used to furnish a house.	....
5 This is the amount of heat shown by a thermometer.	....
6 This is a drawing or painting.	....
7 This word means to take prisoner, or to seize as a prize.	....
8 This is a person's name in his own handwriting.	....
9 This word means a living being.	....
10 When things are mixed together they are said to be this.	....
11 This word means a break. It is used mainly when talking about breaking a bone.	....
12 This means something which is fixed into position. It also means the date of a game, like a football match.	....
13 This word means the making of things, either by hand or by machine.	....
14 This word means something which is made on a small scale.	....

ble, cle, dle

When you see **le** at the end of a word you only say the **l**. The **e** is silent.

(Where there is a double letter, like **bb, dd, rr, ss,** say only one letter.)

ble		cle	dle
able	possible	circle	candle
table	sensible	cycle	handle
stable	responsible	article	needle
vegetable	double	particle	middle
bible	trouble	obstacle	bundle
horrible	bubble	miracle	muddle

A Choose from the words that are underlined.

Clues across

1 Before you add **ed** to the word stop you

must _ _ _ _ _ _ the **p.**

5 Horses are kept in a _ _ _ _ _ _ .

6 You hold a suitcase by the _ _ _ _ _ _ .

7 The centre of a circle is also called

the _ _ _ _ _ _ .

8 The rose is a flower, the carrot is a

_ _ _ _ _ _ _ _ _ .

Clues down

2 Meals are usually laid out on a _ _ _ _ _ .

3 We use a _ _ _ _ _ _ for sewing.

4 I was asked to write an _ _ _ _ _ _ _ on pets for the school magazine.

5 The opposite of silly is _ _ _ _ _ _ _ _ .

B Answer these questions.

1 Can you do this sum? Double 4 + double 2 + double 5 = ...

2 Which articles of clothing do you wear when you go out in the cold

weather? ....

3 What is an obstacle race? ....

fle, gle, ple, tle

> When you see **le** at the end of a word you only say the **l**. The **e** is silent.
>
> (Where there is a double letter, like **ff, gg, pp, tt**, say only one letter.

fle	gle	ple	tle
raffle	angle	apple	battle
rifle	strangle	simple	cattle
duffle	struggle	people	kettle
	smuggle	purple	beetle
	single	example	little
	giggle	couple	title
	jungle		bottle

Choose from the words that are underlined.

Clues across

1 This is one word for human beings.

5 This means : (a) one only (b) not married.

7 This means a fight between large numbers of people.

8 This fruit is green or red-green in colour. You should not eat the core.

10 This is a metal container, with a spout and a handle, used for boiling water.

12 This means:

(a) to fish with hook and bait,

(b) the space between two lines that meet ⌐90°⌐.

13 You buy milk in a carton or a _ _ _ _ _ _ .

14 This means to take goods in or out of a country without paying duty on them.

Clues down

2 The letters e.g. mean for ex _ _ _ _ _ .

3 This means something which is easy to do or to understand.

4 This is an insect that is often found under stones.

6 This means to laugh in a silly way.

9 This means small; not much.

11 One meaning of this word is the name of a book.

ar*

Say the **ar** *like the* **ar** *in* **car.**

In each box there is a group of letters that you will see in all the words below the box.
Say the sound of this group of letters first and then read the words.

ar	ark	arm	art	arp
bar	ark	arm	art	sharp
car	bark	farm	cart	carpet
far	dark	harm	dart	carpenter
jar	mark	army	part	**arch**
tar	market	armour	partner	arch
scar	park	alarm	party	march
star	shark	charming	chart	starch
ard	spark	marmalade	smart	*more words*
card	**arg**	**arge**	start	cigar
hard	argue	barge	**arve**	parcel
yard	argument	charge	carve	farther
garden	cargo	large	harvest	Charles
pardon	target	**arn**	starve	scarf
cardigan		barn	marvellous	scarlet
		varnish		harbour

Complete the sentences by putting the words at the side in the right order.

1	I went to the market yesterday and bought my small sister a	dark smart, dress.	green party
2	My uncle is a carpenter and he likes his	to tools	be sharp.
3	My mother is always telling my brother and	not me	argue. to
4	I spilt some coffee on the carpet yesterday and it	left a	has mark.
5	The army captain, who was in .... started to look for a place to camp for the night.	march, of	charge the
6	The birthday card from my cousin had a charming picture of a	marmalade-coloured on cat front. the

ar followed by e*

| When ar is followed by e it has the sound of the air in chair. |

1	2	3	4	5
bare	fare	Clare	*stare	*compare
*care	hare	*glare	*scare	*prepare
careful	mare	*share	scared	beware
careless	rare	*snare	square	area
*dare	rarely	*spare	parent	
				scarce

A   Change the first letter of the old word to make a new word that fits the new meaning.

old word	meaning of new word	new word
1 care	I mean unclothed or uncovered.	....
2 dare	I mean unusual or uncommon.	....
3 hare	I am the price of a bus ride.	....
4 Clare	I mean to give a fierce stare.	....

Change the second letter in the next two words.

5 stare	I am a trap for animals.	....
6 spare	I mean to frighten.	....

Change the first three letters in the next two words.

7 compare	I mean to make ready.	....
8 beware	I am a shape which has four equal sides and four right angles.	....

B   When you add **ing** to words marked * you cross off the e but still say the ar as air.
Put each word in a sentence: (1) staring (2) glaring (3) preparing.

....

....

....

....

....

ar, and **ar** followed by **e** crossword

Remember: In these words say the **ar** like the **ar** in **car** and the **are** like the **air** in **chair**.

Choose from these words:

army	armour	area	arch	stare
start	share	Scarlet	care	large
bar	parent	tar	argue	spare
arm	rare	part	Star	

Clues across

1 The teacher said, 'You may s _ _ _ _ the exam in two minutes.'

3 When you look at the night sky you can always see the North S _ _ _ because it shines brightly.

5 The new bridge over the river has only one a _ _ _ .

6 In Henry VIII's time the knights wore a _ _ _ _ _ to protect them in battle.

7 One of Robin Hood's men was called Will S _ _ _ _ _ _ . His surname means a bright red colour.

11 Pete and his mother are called a single-p _ _ _ _ _ family because Pete hasn't got a father.

13 My brother and I had a long argument about sharks until Mum told us not to a _ _ _ _ as it was making her head ache.

14 I don't like sweets but sometimes I eat a small b _ _ of chocolate.

15 If you have a pet you must take good _ _ _ _ of it.

Clues down

1 The lady's hat looked so peculiar that all I could do was s _ _ _ _ at it.

2 When I leave school I would like to enlist in the a _ _ _ cadets.

3 When we went to the museum I forgot my lunch but my friend let me s _ _ _ _ hers.

4 Last year a boy from the city of York found an old coin in his garden. The museum said it was a very r _ _ _ Roman coin.

5 15m / 5m The a _ _ _ of this rectangle is 15m x 5m.

8 I asked for a small bag of chips but the man made a mistake and gave me a l _ _ _ _ one instead.

9 My sister had to have her a _ _ in a sling because she broke it when she fell off her bike.

10 We had a puncture yesterday but luckily we had a good s _ _ _ _ tyre.

11 I have the main p _ _ _ in the school play.

12 When men are mending the roads I like to smell the t _ _ .

Some more ar words

When **ar** comes after **w** it says or *as in* **for**.		The **ar** at the end of these words *says* **er** *as in* **butter**.		The **a** *in these words has a short sound.*
1 war warm warn ward	**2** reward towards dwarf swarm	**3** burglar cellar collar vinegar	**4** peculiar popular particular custard sugar	**5** arrive carry caravan ordinary extraordinary

A   Complete the words in the story. Choose from the words in the columns above.

THE CAT BURGLAR

Arthur was a pe _ _ _ _ _ _ man, bad-tempered and unpop _ _ _ _ . He was small and thin with a white bushy beard. I always thought he looked like one of Snow White's dw _ _ _ s. Being small, however, was helpful in his 'job' because he was a b _ _ _ _ _ _ . I say was, because that isn't his job any more. He is now in prison.

As he wasn't a very pop _ _ _ _ person and had few friends nobody visited him in prison. So I decided to pay him a visit. I arr _ _ _ d at two o'clock, and ten minutes later he was telling me this extraordin _ _ _ story.

'This part _ _ _ _ _ _ night,' he said, 'was w _ _ _ and airless and I wished I hadn't worn a c _ _ _ _ _ and tie. After the Reed family had gone out I crept to _ _ _ _ _ the house, climbed up a drainpipe and dropped through a window, carelessly left open, into a back bedroom.

'Ten minutes later, ca _ _ _ ing a bulging bag, I made my way to the ce _ _ _ _ . I crept into the kitchen and shone my torch on the walls to find the c _ _ _ _ _ door. Suddenly everything started to happen.

'I trod on the cat and then put my foot in its bowl of milk. I slipped on the milk and fell over. The cat was very frightened. It jumped onto the fridge and knocked over a bowl of c _ _ _ _ _ _ which fell on my head. The upturned bowl stuck tightly on my head and the c _ _ _ _ _ _ dripped down my neck. As I was struggling to get the bowl off my head the man who lived next door burst in and it was all over for me.

'Later the judge praised the man next door for helping the police catch a b _ _ _ _ _ _ and said he deserved a re _ _ _ _ . Then he said that as I'd had one wa _ _ ing, I would have to go to prison for two years. And here I am.' He looked at me and laughed.

On my way home I laughed too at the thought that Arthur must be the only cat b _ _ _ _ _ _ to have been caught by a cat!

B   Choose one of these titles and write a story:
   (1) The Reward   (2) Caught!   (3) The Secret Door.

or*

Say the **or** in these words like the **or** in **horse**.

or	orm	ort	ore *(The e is silent.)*	harder words
1 <u>for</u> forget forgive <u>horse</u> <u>north</u> <u>story</u> force **ork** fork pork	**2** form <u>storm</u> normal **orn** <u>born</u> corn <u>corner</u> <u>morning</u> **orch** torch orchard	**3** sort <u>short</u> <u>sport</u> forty port export import important	**4** <u>more</u> <u>sore</u> score shore store <u>before</u> <u>explore</u>	**5** decorate evaporate *The o in these words has a different sound.* forest orange sorry

Learn how to spell all the words that are underlined.

What is the word? Find the word in the columns above.	
clues	answers
1 An animal. It sometimes runs in races.	....
2 The opposite of south.	....
3 A place where ships dock.	....
4 Four tens make this number.	....
5 The opposite of long.	....
6 Knife and _ _ _ _ .	....
7 A meat which comes from a pig.	....
8 Many fruit trees.	....
9 This means to bring in goods from other countries.	....
10 This means to send out goods to other countries.	....
11 A small light you can hold in your hand.	....
12 A fruit and a colour.	....

or crossword

Choose from these words:

storm	short	orange
before	story	born
important	score	sore
form	force	for
forest	more	evaporate

Clues across

1 The rain was beating down and I felt glad that I wasn't out in such a bad _ _ _ _ _ .

3 I pushed my brother with such _ _ _ _ _ that he fell over.

6 At half time the _ _ _ _ _ was two goals to one.

7 I always do my homework after dinner but my brother does his homework _ _ _ _ _ _ dinner.

8 I take the dog _ _ _ a walk every day.

10 Some forms ask for your date of birth. This means the date you were _ _ _ _ .

11 In the story *Oliver Twist*, Oliver was hungry so he asked for some _ _ _ _ food.

12 Before you decorate a room it is _ _ _ _ _ _ _ _ _ to cover the carpet or lino.

Clues down

1 My sister wears very high heels because she is so _ _ _ _ _ _ .

2 I like to drink fresh _ _ _ _ _ _ juice.

4 In the Science laboratory we heated water and made it disappear. The teacher said we had made the water _ _ _ _ _ _ _ _ _ .

5 I burned my hand and now it is very _ _ _ _ .

6 My mother or father reads my baby brother a _ _ _ _ _ every night.

8 A big area of woodland is called a _ _ _ _ _ _ .

9 When you go to work full time you have to fill in a tax _ _ _ _ _ .

aw

Say the **aw** *like the* **or** *in* **for.**

1	2	3	4
jaw	claw	lawn	crawl
law	draw	pawn	shawl
paw	straw	prawn	trawler
raw	gnaw	yawn	strawberry
saw	squaw	hawk	awful
outlaw	drawer	lawyer	awkward

Some words that do not follow this rule are: awake, away, aware.

Complete the words with spaces. Choose from the words that are underlined.

HIT AND RUN

The car was going too fast. I s _ _   it hit the dog but it did not stop. 'That's against the l _ _ , 'I said to myself as I ran to help the poor thing.

He had cr _ _ _ ed to the kerb; his p _ _ was bleeding and his j _ _ was hanging open as if it was broken. He was lying awk _ _ _ _ ly and the str _ _ — coloured fur on his neck was wet and matted. I stroked him to comfort him.

A lady in one of the houses must have seen what had happened. She came out with a wet cloth and we cleaned his p _ _ . We then s _ _ that one of his cl _ _ s was broken.

'Just a minute,' the lady said, 'I'll get my woollen sh _ _ _ to make him more comfortable.' She smiled. 'That's if I can find it in one of the dr _ _ _ _ s. They're in such a muddle.'

She came back with the sh _ _ _ and we wrapped him up. He gave what seemed to be a little y _ _ _ and closed his eyes.

We both took him to see the vet. The people waiting told us to go in first.

'Poor little fellow,' the vet said after we told him about the aw _ _ _ hit and run driver. 'Never mind, old son, we'll look after you. You'll soon be gn _ _ ing those bones again.' He looked at me, 'His owners will claim him in the next few days. I hope this will teach them not to let their pet roam the streets by himself!'

Make up a play called Waiting for the Vet. *Think of all the different people in the waiting room and the sort of conversation they might have about their pets.*

aw crossword

All the words in this crossword contain the letters **aw**.

Choose from these words:

outlaw	raw	draw
strawberry	claw	lawn
hawk	yawn	straw
trawler	awkward	jaw
paws	saw	aw

Clues across

1 You can drink Coke through this.

2 This is the name for the grass in the garden.

4 Robin Hood was an _ _ _ law.

8 This is another word for uncooked.

9 This is a bird of prey, like an eagle.

10 The first two letters of the word awful.

13 You do this with a pencil.

14 You do this sometimes when you're tired.

Clues down

1 This is a red fruit (_ _ _ _ _ berry).

3 This is the pointed nail on a bird's foot.

5 This is a fishing boat. The fish are caught with a trawl net.

6 This is another word for clumsy. It begins with awk _ _ _ _ .

7 Our teeth are set in this part of the face.

11 This is used to cut wood.

12 This is the name of the feet of a cat or dog.

oi (1)

When **o** and **i** come together in a word they sound like the **o** in **on** and the **i** in **in**. The two sounds are blended together but both vowels can be heard.

1	2	3	4	5
oil	coin	point	noise	In these words the **oi** has different sounds.
boil	join	appoint	noisy	
coil	joint	appointment	poison	
foil	choice	disappoint	hoist	
soil	voice	ointment	joist	choir
spoil	avoid		moist	reservoir
toilet	turquoise		moisture	tortoise

A   Complete the words with spaces. Choose from the words that are underlined.

BOB'S STORY

Our ap _ _ _ _ _ _ _ _ _ with Mrs Hardy was for 10.00 am and at 9.45 I was still waiting upstairs in my office for Harry to turn up with the tools. Mrs Hardy, our client, wanted two j _ _ _ _ s in the loft renewed, but she had already p _ _ _ ted out that 10.00 am meant ten o'clock in the morning and not 12 o'clock noon, like last time.

'That Harry,' I said to myself. 'If he oversleeps again I'll . . . . . 'At that moment the door slammed, a v _ _ _ _ boomed out a greeting and a clattering n _ _ _ _ on the stairs told me that Harry had arrived.

He puffed into the room, beads of sweat shining on his face. He wiped away the m _ _ _ _ _ _ _ with a grubby hand and smiled.

'Kettle on the b _ _ _ , is it?' I had to laugh.

'Sorry to dis _ _ _ _ _ _ _ you, pal. We're late already,' I said.

'It won't sp _ _ _ your morning if you don't have a fifth cup of tea, will it?' Harry pretended to think. Then he said,

'Well it doesn't look as if I'll have a chance, does it?' I was gripping him by the arm by this time and pulling him out of the office.

'Just a minute.' He rushed back inside. 'I've got to go to the t _ _ _ _ _ first. I'll j _ _ _ you downstairs.'

continued on page L2

oi (2)

continued from page L1

As he disappeared through the door I moaned silently.

'F _ _ led again,' I thought and sat down on the stairs.

Another lot of banging and clattering woke me into action. 'Hurry up,' I roared angrily.

Harry appeared still h _ _ _ ting up his trousers.

'Are we all ready now?' he asked. I looked at his happy face and my bad mood

evaporated. Harry was a kind man and a very good carpenter. We would not be all that

late for Mrs Hardy.

B Answer these questions. Write in sentences.

1 What time was Bob and Harry's appointment with Mrs Hardy? ....

2 How do you know Bob and Harry had been late before for an appointment with

Mrs Hardy? ....

3 How do you know that Harry was often late? ....

....

4 Which sentence tells you that Harry liked tea? ....

....

5 Why do you think Bob wasn't angry in the end? ....

....

C Complete these sentences.

1 A choir is ....

2 A reservoir is ....

3 A tortoise is ....

4 Turquoise is ....

5 Another word for soil is ....

D Read Harry's story on the oy worksheet (page L3), then see if you can act the story. You may have to invent some more characters. Add a good ending.

oy

When o and y come together in a word they are sounded like the o in on and the i in in.
The two sounds are blended together but both vowels can be heard.

1	2	3	4
			harder words
<u>boy</u>	<u>annoy</u>	<u>royal</u>	alloy
joy	<u>destroy</u>	royalty	decoy
<u>enjoy</u>	destroyer	employ	<u>convoy</u>
toy	loyal	<u>employer</u>	oyster
	<u>loyalty</u>	employee	voyage
		<u>employment</u>	

A   Complete the words with spaces. Choose from the words that are underlined.

HARRY'S STORY

I could hear Bob shouting at me, 'Hurry up, Harry!' I knew I had a _ _ _ _ ed him

by making us late for our appointment with Mrs Hardy. 'He's a good em _ _ _ _ _ _ ,' I

thought. 'I must try to be a better em _ _ _ _ ee or one day soon I'll be looking for other

em _ _ _ _ ment.'

'Are we all ready now?' I smiled. I didn't want to des _ _ _ _ a good partnership.

Thank goodness he returned the smile.

'Come on, my b _ _ , let's get going before there's no morning left to en _ _ _ .'

We ran down the stairs and away we sped in the van. It just wasn't my day, however;

for we were soon jammed behind a con _ _ _ of huge lorries. Nobody seemed to be in any

great hurry and I could just see us losing the Hardy job.

We needn't have worried. Mrs Hardy, who is a journalist on our local paper, was

writing an article about the Roy _ _ Family and didn't have to go into her office.

She showed us the joists we had to replace and we agreed to do the work immediately.

What happened next is another story.

B   Complete these sentences. Use your dictionary to help you.

An employee is

....

A convoy is

....

Loyalty means

....

oi and oy

A	What am I?

Choose from these words:

toys	coins	oyster	poison	destroyer	joint
voyage	noise	soil	alloy	oil	point

clues	answers
1 Most children play with me.	....
2 I am another name for the tip of a pencil.	....
3 I am used to stop doors and wheels squeaking.	....
4 I am a shell fish.	....
5 You pay for your comics with me.	....
6 You will die if you drink me.	....
7 I am a warship.	....
8 I am dark brown. You put plants in me.	....
9 You must make me properly in your woodwork lesson.	....
10 I am a long journey.	....
11 I am a mixture of two or more metals.	....
12 I am another name for sound.	....

B	Put each word in a sentence: (1) voice (2) avoid (3) employer (4) annoy.

....

....

....

....

....

....

....

ow; long ō

<table>
<tr><td colspan="6">Say the ow like the ow in arrow. »»»——————→</td></tr>
<tr><td>1</td><td>2</td><td>3</td><td>4</td><td>5</td></tr>
<tr><td>bow</td><td>grow</td><td>show</td><td>arrow</td><td>yellow</td></tr>
<tr><td>low</td><td>blow</td><td>snow</td><td>barrow</td><td>window</td></tr>
<tr><td>mow</td><td>flow</td><td>know</td><td>marrow</td><td>pillow</td></tr>
<tr><td>row</td><td>glow</td><td>throw</td><td>narrow</td><td>hollow</td></tr>
<tr><td>sow</td><td>slow</td><td>elbow</td><td>sparrow</td><td>follow</td></tr>
<tr><td>tow</td><td>owe</td><td>below</td><td>shallow</td><td>borrow</td></tr>
<tr><td>crow</td><td>own</td><td>bowl</td><td>fellow</td><td>tomorrow</td></tr>
</table>

A *Change the first letter of the old word to make a new word that fits the new meaning.*

old word	new meaning	new word
1 bow	This is the opposite of high.	....
2 tow	This means to put seed in the ground.	....
3 row	This means to cut the grass.	....
4 crow	This means to get bigger or taller.	....
5 glow	This means not quick.	....
6 know	This is white and falls as flakes in winter.	....
7 flow	This means to make a current of air: When the north winds _ _ _ _ we shall have snow.	....
8 marrow	This is the opposite of wide.	....
9 fellow	This is a colour.	....
10 follow	This means not solid but empty inside.	....

B *How many words can you make out of the word in the rectangle?*
You may also use the letter in the triangle.

1	shallow + △t	....
2	tomorrow + △b	....
3	window + △k	....

ow as in cow

Say the **ow** like the **ow** in **cow**.

1	2	3	4	5
bow	sow	brown	howl	flower
cow	allow	drown	growl	shower
how	eyebrows	crown	prowl	crowd
however	down	frown	towel	powder
now	downstairs	clown	vowel	coward
row	town	owl	powder	cowboy
			tower	

A Change the first letter of the old word to make a new word that fits the new meaning.

old word	new meaning	new word
1 now	This animal gives us the milk we drink.	....
2 how	This word means a lot of noise, or a quarrel.	....
3 down	This has many houses. It is larger than a village and smaller than a city.	....
4 brown	This is worn on the head of a king or a queen.	....
5 prowl	When a dog is angry it makes this noise.	....
6 frown	This means to die by being kept under water.	....
7 vowel	We dry ourselves with this.	....
8 power	This is a tall building like the _ _ _ _ _ of London.	....

B Put each word in a sentence: (1) town (2) brown (3) towel (4) crowd.

....

....

....

....

....

....

ow crossword

Choose from these words:

brown	window	crowd
tomorrow	narrow	bowl
owe	grow	low
slow	own	throw
arrow	now	

Clues across

1 My mother puts fruit in a big glass

_ _ _ _ .

2 My dog likes me to _ _ _ _ _

sticks for him to fetch.

4 One day I would like to _ _ _ a big car.

5 There was a _ _ _ _ _ of people waiting for tickets to the football game.

6 A new sports shop is _ _ _ open in the town.

8 The clown bowed _ _ _ at the end of his act.

10 In Devon some roads are so _ _ _ _ _ _ that two cars can't pass at the same time.

11 Many oak trees _ _ _ _ in our forests.

12 The 9.15 train to York is the fast train. Don't take the 9.30 train because it's the _ _ _ _

one.

Clues down

1 My father's hair is black, my mother's hair is blonde and I have _ _ _ _ _ hair.

2 Today is 31st December and _ _ _ _ _ _ _ _ is the start of a new year.

3 I kicked my football and it went through the kitchen _ _ _ _ _ _ by mistake.

7 In the Middle Ages men used to fight with a bow and _ _ _ _ _ .

9 I borrowed another 50p from my brother and I now _ _ _ him £1.

ou as in cloud*

Say the **ou** like the **ou** in **cloud**.

1	2	3	4	5
out	round	count	ounce	thousand
about	around	counter	bounce	our
outside	surround	amount	pounce	hour
shout	sound	fountain	announce	sour
found	loud	mountain	house	flour
pound	aloud	noun	mouse	mouth
ground	cloud	foul	blouse	south
mound	proud	doubt	trousers	

A Change the first letter of the old word to make a new word that fits the new meaning.

	old word	new meaning	new word
1	round	This equals one hundred pence.	....
2	sound	This is the past tense of the word find.	....
3	around	Nottingham Forest's football .... is called The City.	....
4	aloud	This is in the sky. If it is black or grey we may have rain.	....
5	fountain	This is a very high hill.	....
6	house	This is a tiny animal with a long tail. Cats try to catch it.	....
7	hour	This is the opposite of sweet.	....
8	mouth	This is one of the points of the compass: north, ... , east, west.	
9	bounce	This means to spring at and seize: A cat will .... on a mouse.	....

B Complete these sentences using your own words.
Try to use a word containing **ou** in each sentence.

1 I found ....

2 Snowdon is ....

3 Our house ....

4 The sound ....

ou as in cloud crossword

Choose from these words:

thousand	mouth
mountains	shout
our	sound
trousers	proud
ounce	count
foul	hours
sour	out
ground	south

Clues across

1 These are very high hills.

5 This word means belonging to us: We are having a party in _ _ _ house.

6 This is a loud cry. It also means to speak loudly.

8 There are twenty-four of these in one whole day.

10 This is a point of the compass. It is opposite north.

12 This is the surface of the earth: I would not like to be a miner and work below _ _ _ _ _ _ .

13 This word means to reckon up or to say numbers in order.

14 One meaning of this word is 'against the rules': The referee said the footballer had committed a _ _ _ _ when he kicked the centre-half.

Clues down

1 Your tongue and your teeth are inside this.

2 You multiply 100 by 10 to obtain this number.

3 This is another name for a noise and begins with s.

4 This word means feeling or showing pride in something: I felt _ _ _ _ _ when I was chosen for the tennis team.

6 This word means something that is not sweet: This apple is not ripe and is very _ _ _ _ _ .

7 This is the bottom half of a suit.

9 This is a unit of weight.

11 This word means the opposite of in.

The different sound of **ea** and **ei** (1)

In these words **ea** *and* **ei** *do not say* **ē**.
They have the sounds that are in the boxes above the words.

ea				ei
1 short ĕ	**2** short ĕ	**3** short ĕ	**4** long ā	**5** long ā *(The gh is silent.)*
head	thread	pleasure	steak	eight
dead	threat	treasure	break	freight
read	death	weapon	great	weight
ready	breath	weather	*The ea sounds like the* **ur** *in* **church.**	sleigh
already	heavy	feather		weigh
instead	deaf	leather		neighbour
dreadful	breakfast	sweat	earn	reign
bread	health	sweater	learn	vein
tread	pleasant	*The ear says air.*	early	short ĕ
spread		wear	earth	leisure
			search	short ĭ silent g
			rehearse	foreign

Complete the words in the story. Choose from the words that are underlined.

BREAKFAST CONVERSATION

We were having our br _ _ _ _ _ _ _ yesterday when Mum r _ _ d in the paper that the price of br _ _ _ was going up.

'It's alr _ _ _ _ a dear food,' she said. 'Dad, you'll have to ea _ _ more if we want br _ _ d for br _ _ _ _ _ _ _ , let along anything to spr _ _ _ on it. And what happened to the gr _ _ _ British breakfast of bacon and egg?' she continued. 'Let alone the price of st _ _ _ _ .'

Dad just grunted and I looked up.

'Well, if you don't eat much you won't have a w _ _ _ _ t problem, will you, Mum?' I said.

'Jane w _ _ ghs herself every day,' she went on.

'Who?' I asked.

'Our n _ _ _ _ bour, Mrs Johns.'

'What's that got to do with the price of br _ _ _ ?' She ignored this. 'Poor food is the cause of bad h _ _ _ th. Your friend gets all those h _ _ _ y colds because he doesn't eat the right food.'

'That's not true, Mum.' I looked at the clock. Dad, it's ei _ _ _ o'clock alr _ _ _ _ ,' I said. Dad went on reading. 'Dad,' I shouted, 'are you d _ _ _ ? It's ei _ _ _ o'clock!'

'Yes, hurry up, dear,' Mum said. She got up and went to the window. 'The w _ _ th _ _ doesn't look very promising. We _ _ that thick sw _ _ t _ _ today.'

Dad seemed to take ages to get r _ _ _ _ . Mum had alr _ _ _ _ forgotten about the price of bread (and f _ _ _ _ gn cars, which was yesterday's subject).

continued on page L11

The different sounds of **ea** and **ei** (2)

continued from page L10

She had to go to work herself so she liked to see us off on time.

As we went out Mum called, 'Have a pl _ _ _ _ _ _ day, and be home ear _ _ .'

Dad and I looked at each other and grinned.

'Okay,' we both said. 'See you.'

Another day had begun.

Choose from these words

bread	Death	search
ready	health	early
feather	heavy	eight
wear	break	weight
weather	great	neighbour
breath	earth	height

Clues across

1 When you go on holiday you hope that the _ _ _ _ _ _ _ will be fine.

3 _ _ _ _ _ is made from flour and water, it is made into a dough and baked.

6 The person who lives next door to you is called your _ _ _ _ _ _ _ _ _ .

7 The measurement from the bottom to the top of anything is called the _ _ _ _ _ _ _ .

10 Cross off the l in leather and put an f instead. Now you have the word _ _ _ _ _ _ _ _ .

12 The air which you take into and let out of your lungs is called your _ _ _ _ _ _ _ .

14 The opposite of late is _ _ _ _ _ .

15 Something 'of great weight' is very _ _ _ _ _ .

16 When your body and mind are sound and fit we say you are in good _ _ _ _ _ _ _ .

Clues down

1 The amount anything weighs is its _ _ _ _ _ _ .

2 Two multiplied by four equals _ _ _ _ _ .

4 Another name for soil is _ _ _ _ _ . It is also the name of the planet on which we live.

5 Many Londoners died in the plague of 1665 which was called the Black _ _ _ _ _ .

8 The word _ _ _ _ _ means large, important or famous.

9 If you want to find something you have lost you have to _ _ _ _ _ _ for it.

11 A race does not begin until all the athletes are _ _ _ _ _ .

12 If you fall and _ _ _ _ _ your arm you might have to wear a sling.

13 When the weather is cold you should _ _ _ _ warm clothing.

The different sounds of ie, ui, ua, and ue

The different sounds of ie, ui, ua and ue are in the boxes above the words.

ie			ui	ua and ue
1 long ē	**2** long ē	**3** long ē	**4** short ĭ	**5** like the ar in **star** ✦
field	belief	yield	build	guard
shield	disbelief	believe	building	short ă
brief	handkerchief	achieve	built	guarantee
grief	niece	fierce	guilt	short ĕ
chief	piece	short ĭ	guilty	guess
thief	priest	sieve	guitar	guest
relief	siege	short ĕ	long ī	
		friend	guide	
			disguise	

Complete the words in the story. Choose from the words that are underlined.

THE SIEGE

The s _ _ _ _ was eight months old when I arrived. My father hugged me. 'Thank God you came.' He sighed deeply with rel _ _ _ . 'They will not y _ _ _ _ ,' he said. 'I bel _ _ _ _ they have God's hand to gu _ _ _ them. We have ach _ _ _ _ d nothing in these past months.'

I looked across the battlef _ _ _ _ to the tall bu _ _ _ _ _ _ s beyond the massive walls. 'Yes, bu _ lt to serve them well,' I thought and added aloud, 'How many soldiers g _ _ _ _ the walls at night, Father?'

'We can only g _ _ ss the numbers by the glint of moonlight on their swords and sh _ _ _ _ s. Certainly over half the army g _ _ _ _ the walls each night.'

'Do you ever see their king?'

He laughed bitterly. 'No, he fears a sudden attack. Yesterday, though, we saw their ch _ _ _ pr _ _ _ _ on the walls.'

'Did he bless their army?' I asked.

'One of our men, disg _ _ _ ed as a shepherd, moved closer to the walls. The pr _ _ _ _ called upon God and some time later the Great God answered with thunder and lightning over the sea.'

He said nothing for a few moments. Suddenly his fi _ _ _ _ looking face softened and tears came into his eyes. 'Pelemon is dead,' he said sadly.

I stared at him in disb _ _ _ _ _ . I couldn't answer. Pelemon, my brother, the best friend I'd ever had. His happy life had been all too br _ _ f. 'Yes,' I thought, 'God is definitely on their side.'

Have you read the story of the siege of Troy? The Greeks besieged the city for ten years until they gained entry by a trick. Do you know how the Greeks tricked the Trojans?

The soft sound of g; g before e*

When g *comes* before e *it usually has a soft sound like the* j *in* **jam.**				

1	2	3	4	5
age	hinge	large	geography	danger
cage	fringe	charge	geometry	legend
page	huge	gem	George	suggest
rage	change	germ	Germany	tragedy
wage	strange	general	agent	vegetables
stage		gentle	urgent	

Answer these questions.

1 What is your age? .... years .... months.

2 What is a weekly wage? ....

3 (a) Does **huge** mean the same as **very large**? ....

   (b) Put the word huge in a sentence of your own. ....

   ....

4 If a letter is marked **urgent** what does this mean? ....

   ....

5 (a) Find Germany and Switzerland on a map. Is Germany larger than Switzerland?

   | Yes | | No | Tick the right answer.

   (b) Name two other countries that border Germany. ....

6 Draw and name your four favourite vegetables.

   ....

7 Underline the correct sentence: (a) A tragedy is a happy event.

   (b) A tragedy is a sad event.

8 (a) Underline the words that mean the same as **strange:** rage, odd, suggest, fringe, unusual.

   (b) Draw a strange animal. Write a short story about this animal.

The soft sound of g; g before i and y*

When g *comes before* i *or* y *it sometimes has a soft sound like the* j *in* jam.			
g before i			**g before y**
1 giant gin ginger giraffe	**2** magic tragic magistrate register	**3** apologise religion region engine	**4** gypsy (or gipsy) gym apology energy

What am I?

clues	answers
1 I am an African animal with a long neck and very long legs.	....
2 I am a light reddish-yellow colour. I am also a spice.	....
3 I am a huge, super-human person. You find me in fairy stories and legends.	....
4 I am a person before whom some court cases are tried.	....
5 I am a word meaning conjuring or witchcraft.	....
6 I am a person who likes to live in a caravan and move around the countryside.	....
7 I am a room for physical education — P.E. My long name is gymnasium.	....
8 I am a word meaning to make an apology.	....
9 I am a large area or district: The hottest .... of the world is on the equator.	....
10 I am a word meaning force or power: Food gives you	....
11 I am a list of names.	....
12 I pull the carriages of a train.	....

The soft sound of g*

age at the end of 2 - or 3 - syllable words			
Say the **age** *at the end of these words as* **ij.**			
1 bandage cabbage cottage damage garage	**2** luggage manage manager message package postage	**3** passage shortage stoppage village voyage hostage	**4** courage savage average advantage carriage marriage

Answer these questions.

1 What is the postage for a first class letter? ....

2 What is another name for a voyage? ....

3 Do you think it is an advantage to have a garage if you own a car? ....

Why? ....

4 If John is 6 years old, Mary is 9 years old and Sam is 15 years old,

what is their average age? ....

5 Why do you think there are notices in some train carriages saying, 'Danger. Look out for

luggage and packages left unattended'? ....

....

6 Your mother urgently needs a bandage because she has cut herself very badly. You run to

the chemist's and he charges you £1.65p for a large bandage. If you give him a £5 note how

much change will you be given? ....

7 What is a village? ....

8 Draw a cottage, with cabbages growing in the vegetable garden at the side.

The soft sound of g; g before e crossword

Choose from these words

urgent	cage	change
cottage	garage	stage
general	rage	danger
gentle	agent	age
large	manage	wage
luggage	suggest	

Clues across

1 When you pay for something in a shop you must look carefully at your _ _ _ _ _ _ .

6 I sent a letter to my son asking him to come home at once as his father was very ill. I marked the letter _ _ _ _ _ _ .

8 I think I might be an actor and go on the _ _ _ _ _ when I leave school.

9 I don't get into a terrible temper now because when I was little my father took no notice of me when I got into a _ _ _ _ .

12 Most children start school at the _ _ _ of five.

13 You have to be very _ _ _ _ _ _ with a newborn baby.

15 If you want to leave your suitcases somewhere when you arrive at a main-line station you can leave them in the left _ _ _ _ _ _ _ office.

Clues down

1 Our pet hamster has a new _ _ _ _ .

2 My father's car would not start in the cold weather and he said he wished he had a _ _ _ _ _ _ .

3 I'd like to live in a small _ _ _ _ _ _ _ with a large garden.

4 When I go to work I'd like a weekly _ _ _ _ and not a monthly one.

5 My teacher says I have a good _ _ _ _ _ _ _ knowledge.

7 When the water freezes in the lake notices are put up saying, ' _ _ _ _ _ _ . Thin ice.'

8 When I told my father that I didn't have anything to do he said, 'I _ _ _ _ _ _ _ you do your homework!'

10 James Bond was a very good secret _ _ _ _ _ .

11 My mother said she could never _ _ _ _ _ _ without her washing machine.

14 I asked the man for a _ _ _ _ _ ice-cream but he said he only had small tubs left.

dge*

dge *has the sound of a soft* g, *like the* j *in* jam.				
ă**dge**	ĕ**dge**	ĭ**dge**	ŏ**dge**	ŭ**dge**
1	**2**	**3**	**4**	**5**
badge	edge	bridge	dodge	fudge
	hedge	fridge	lodge	judge
badger	ledge	ridge		nudge
gadget	sledge	porridge	lodger	smudge
	wedge			
		fidget		budget
	knowledge	midget		

Complete each sentence by using the right word or words from the box at the side.	
1 The .... on my jacket says 'Love everybody'.	budget badge badger
2 After I put milk on my .... I placed the bottle of milk back in the	fridge ridge porridge
3 I bought some .... from the sweet shop.	nudge fidget fudge
4 The .... sentenced the man to three years in prison.	smudge judge edge
5 It snowed yesterday and we took our .... to the park.	sledge wedge hedge
6 The notice on the cliffs said, 'Danger. Do not go near the cliff ....'	ledge dodge edge
7 There were many shops on the old, 13th-century London .... (Can you find a picture of this bridge?)	midget bridge fridge
8 My mother has an electric mixer and many other .... in her kitchen.	budgets gadgets midgets
9 My father asked me to help him cut the garden	knowledge hedge edge
10 I had to .... behind a hedge to avoid meeting my brother.	badge dodge lodger

The soft sound of c; c before e at the end of a word

*When **c** comes before **e** it has a soft sound like the **s** in **sit**.*

easy words			harder words	
1	**2**	**3**	**4**	**5**
ace	ice	notice	dance	scarce
face	dice	office	chance	voice
race	mice	officer	choice	distance
place	nice	police	fierce	entrance
space	rice	practice	force	absence
trace	price	prince	juice	offence
fence	slice	since	niece	sentence
pence	twice	once	piece	difference
silence	advice		peace	service

Complete each sentence by putting the words at the side in the right order.

1 The ....

.... is twice as much now as it was last year.

price	bread
of	sliced

2 It snowed all Friday morning but by Saturday morning there wasn't a

....

snow.	or
	of
ice	trace

3 What had once been an open space was now fenced in and there was a

big ....

.... that said, 'Trespassers will be prosecuted.'

by	notice
entrance	the

4 I went to the Careers Office to get some ....

.... of jobs.

choice	the
advice	on

5 My niece's dog was very fierce, but since she has taken him to a

training centre ....

.... now he is a very gentle dog.

notice	you
the difference;	

6 Before sentence was passed on the prisoner the judge thanked the
police officer for his courage in disarming such a violent criminal. 'In my
experience, men like Officer Price are scarce these days,' he said.

'This officer is a credit ....

the	force.'
police	to

7 I like to do ....
the dining room but Dad says he likes a bit of peace in the evening so
I do my practice in my bedroom.

my	practice
violin	in

When you have finished, read these sentences to your teacher.

The soft sound of c; c before e; difficult words*

When c comes before e it has a soft sound like the s in sit. When two cs* come before e say the first c as a k and the second c as an s.

1	2	3	4	5
cell	ceiling	concentrate	grocer	December
cellar	cement	concern	receive	necessary
celebrate	cereal	concert	receipt	licence
cent	ceremony	excellent	recent	*accept
centre	certain	except	innocent	*accelerate
central	certainly	exceed	produce	*success
century	certificate	experience	cancelled	insurance

Complete each sentence by putting the words at the side in the right order.

1	The recent rise in the television .... mean that some people will not be able to afford a television licence.	fee certainly	licence will
2	In Marks and Spencer's you have to .... you want to change anything that costs over a certain amount.	produce a	if receipt
3	With all this rain my father is very concerned that our roof will leak again and the	will ceiling	bedroom collapse.
4	My driving instructor said that after I pass my test I must always .... with me in case I ever have to produce it for the police.	carry my	driving licence
5	My mother bought me a new watch .... in the exams.	to celebrate	success my
6	I went back to school to .... at the prize-giving ceremony.	receive my	exam certificates
7	If, when you are driving a car, you .... and are caught, you will be fined.	the limit	speed exceed
8	The concert on 8th December at the Arts'	Centre was	suddenly cancelled.

c before e crossword

Choose from these words:

notice	fierce	receipt
twice	certainly	ace
piece	centre	choice
ice	juice	voice
niece	cell	

Clues across

1 Someone asks you for help. If you are certain that you can help you might say, ' _ _ _ _ _ _ _ _ _ '.

5 You pin notices on a _ _ _ _ _ _ board.

6 This playing card counts as one. This word also means someone who excels in a sport or a skill: _ _ _ .

7 When you pay for your goods in a shop you receive a _ _ _ _ _ _ _ for your money.

11 If you visit someone who is very ill you should try to speak in a soft _ _ _ _ _ .

12 Your brother's or sister's daughter is called your _ _ _ _ _ .

13 In a prison the small room a prisoner sleeps in is called a _ _ _ _ .

Clues down

1 The word _ _ _ _ _ _ means in the middle.

2 When something is done two times we say it is done _ _ _ _ _ .

3 When water freezes it turns into _ _ _ .

4 Another word for savage is _ _ _ _ _ _ .

8 If you want to choose a record for your birthday you might say, 'May I have my own _ _ _ _ _ _ of record, please?'

9 The word _ _ _ _ _ means a bit or part of something.

10 When I am thirsty I like to drink fresh orange _ _ _ _ _ .

The soft sound of c; c before i*

When c comes before i *it has a soft sound like the* s *in* sit.
When two cs * come before i *say the first* c *as a* k *and the second* c *as an* s.

1	2	3	4
city	circumference	exciting	electricity
citizen	civil	exercise	society
cinema	civilisation	science	recipe
cider	decide	scientist	vacancies
cigarette	decimal	disciple	*accident
circus	pencil	medicine	*vaccination
circle	council		

True or false (untrue)?	answer
1 The circumference of a circle is the distance all round the outside edge.	....
2 Cider is a drink made from plums.	....
3 Smoking cigarettes can damage your health.	....
4 A recipe is a type of food.	....
5 You can see acrobats and clowns in a circus.	....
6 You can still see remains of the Roman civilisation in Britain. Hadrian's Wall in the north of England is a good example.	....
7 Electricity was first used in the home when two scientists, called Thomas Edison and Joseph Swann, invented the electric light bulb.	....
8 If you see this sign outside a factory it means people are needed to fill these jobs. VACANCIES Machinists Cutters	....
9 In Britain we use decimal currency (money).	....

The soft sound of c; c before y*

When c comes before y it has a soft sound like the s in sit.

Say the y like a long ī	Say the y like a short ĭ	Say the y like a long ē	
1 Cyprus cycle cyclist cyclone	**2** bicycle cylinder cygnet	**3** mercy fancy policy currency	**4** agency emergency urgency democracy vacancy

1   Draw the island of Cyprus.

Find Cyprus on a map and complete these sentences.

(a)   Cyprus is situated in the M .... Sea.

(b)   The northern coast of Cyprus is near the country of T ....

2   A cygnet is a baby swan.

Its feathers are light brown.   Draw a cygnet.

3   Employment Agency has vacancy for an office junior. Good pay and prospects. Telephone: 321-7381

← Where might you see this advertisement? ....

....

4   This is a cylinder.

Copy the diagram here. →

5   Draw a picture of a bicycle. Then look up **bi** in the dictionary and complete this sentence: It is called a <u>bi</u>cycle because

....

6   **EMERGENCY EXIT**

Copy this sign exactly then write where you might see a sign like it.

....

7   **Holiday Insurance Policy**
Name........................ Age........
Personal Accident....................
....£1,000
Luggage and money....................
....£600
Medical expenses....................
....£10,000

If you go abroad for a holiday why should you take

out a holiday insurance policy? ....

....

c before i and y crossword

Choose from these words:

exercise	circle
recipe	decide
cinema	pencil
emergency	city
civil	cycle
policy	science
electricity	exciting

Clues across

1 The James Bond books are always very _ _ _ _ _ _ _ _ .

4 The _ _ _ _ of London chooses a new Lord Mayor every year.

7 My mother baked a fancy chocolate cake. 'It's a new _ _ _ _ _ _ ,' she said.

8 We are learning about the _ _ _ _ _ rights movement in America.

9 I went to see an exciting film at the _ _ _ _ _ _ .

11 There was a terrible accident in the High Street. One man was taken to hospital for an _ _ _ _ _ _ _ _ _ operation.

12 We are not allowed to write in _ _ _ _ _ _ in our school.

13 The price of gas is nearly as high as the price of _ _ _ _ _ _ _ _ _ _ _ .

Clues down

1 My father is getting fat and his doctor said he needed plenty of _ _ _ _ _ _ _ _ and less food.

2 The Maths teacher asked us to find the circumference of a _ _ _ _ _ _ .

3 I _ _ _ _ _ to school as I don't live very far away.

5 My mother asked me when we had to _ _ _ _ _ _ which subjects we were going to take in the fourth year.

6 I am taking exams in all the _ _ _ _ _ _ _ subjects because I want to study medicine when I leave school.

10 My father had a bad accident when we were in Spain. He said he was glad he had taken out a good insurance _ _ _ _ _ _ .

Silent letters; kn, gn

When k and g come before n they are silent and only the n is sounded.

kn		gn	
1	**2**	**3**	**4**
knack	knob	gnash	consignment
knee	knock	gnat	campaign
kneel	knockout	gnaw	foreign
knew	knot	gnome	reign
knife	know	sign	
knight	knowledge	design	
knit	knuckles	resign	

Complete the words with spaces. Choose from the words that are underlined.

kn

1 My mother has the _ _ _ ck of cutting herself whenever she sharpens a _ _ _ fe.

2 I _ _ _ w how to tie many different _ _ _ ts.

3 The boxer sank slowly to his _ _ _ es and then fell forward onto his face. 'It's a

_ _ _ _ _ out!' shouted the referee.

4 My mother polishes our door _ _ _ b and door _ _ _ _ _ er every day.

5 My sister is going to _ _ _ t me a new sweater.

6 I _ _ _ e _ all the answers in the quiz and my teacher said I had a good general

_ _ _ _ _ le _ _ _ .

gn

1 The man gave a sharp whistle which was a s _ _ _ to the dog that he could start to

_ _ _ w his bone.

2 I like the des _ _ _ of that new for _ _ _ _ car.

3 The customs men found a cons _ _ _ _ _ _ _ t of for_ _ _ _ guns hidden in the hold of

the ship.

4 Queen Victoria rei _ _ ed for sixty-four years.

5 Some people put tiny plastic gn _ _ _ s in their gardens.

6 My mother had to res _ _ _ from her job in London because my father has a new job in

Birmingham.

Silent letters; wr, mb

| When w comes before r it is silent and only the r is sounded. |||||
| When b comes after m it is silent and only the m is sounded. |||||

wr		mb	
1	**2**	**3**	**4**
wrap	wrinkle	lamb	crumb
wreath	wrist	bomb	dumb
wreck	write	comb	numb
wrench	writer	tomb	thumb
wrestle	wrong	climb	plumber
wriggle	wrote	limb	
wring	wrung		

Complete the words with spaces. Choose from the words that are underlined.

wr

1   My father said I was _ _ _ ng not to _ _ _ te a postcard to my mother when I went on

the school journey.

2   I _ _ _ _ ped my friend's Christmas present in pretty paper.

3   The thief _ _ _ _ ched the wages bag from the Security man's _ _ ist.

4   The diver _ _ _ ggled through the porthole of the sunken _ _ _ ck.

5   The old lady's face was very _ _ _ _ kled.

6   I _ _ _ te eighteen pages on the History topic entitled 'Knights of the Middle Ages'.

mb

1   The pl _ _ _ _ _ had to cl _ _ _ up into the loft to examine the burst water pipe.

2   I hit my th _ _ _ with the hammer by accident and it went n _ _ _ .

3   The pyramids were the t _ _ _ s of the pharaohs of Egypt.

4   When it is very cold the farmers have to make sure that the newborn l _ _ _ s do not die.

5   On 6th August 1945 the first atomic _ _ _ _ was dropped on Hiroshima in Japan.

6   You must not c _ _ _ your hair when you are preparing food.

More silent letters*

Here are some more words with silent letters.
Use a coloured pencil to underline the silent letter in each word.

1	2	3	4
calm	debt	honest	receipt
palm	doubt	exhaust	scissors
half	sword	exhausted	ascend
column	answer	vehicle	descend
solemn	iron	listen	scene
autumn	hour	fasten	island

Complete the words in the story. Choose from the words that are underlined.

FLIGHT TO AMERICA

This year my father won some money and we all decided to go for an a _ _ _ _ _ holiday to my aunty's house in New Haven near New York.

We wanted to visit her last year but Dad said he wasn't getting into d _ _ _ just for a holiday.

So on 10th October we left from Heathrow airport at h _ _ _ past ten in the morning. To be hon _ _ _ , as we climbed up the steps and into the plane, I had a few dou _ _ s and felt a little scared.

We found our seats. Then we l _ _ _ _ ned to a stewardess giving instructions about the emergency exits, life jackets and oxygen supply. A lighted sign told us not to smoke and to f _ _ _ _ _ our seat belts.

The plane taxied onto the runway and in seconds we were off. It sped along and then seemed to as _ _ _ _ almost vertically. I tried to keep ca _ _ but when I looked at Dad he was very so _ _ _ _ . 'Are you all right, Dad?' I asked. He was too busy wiping the p _ _ _ s of his hands to an _ _ _ _ and I realised that he was scared too. Only Mum looked relaxed and happy, and when she smiled at me I felt better.

The flight took six h _ _ _ _ . I had slept for some of the time but as the plane began to d _ _ _ _ _ _ I still felt ex _ _ _ _ _ _ _ _ . I looked out of the window. The sc _ _ _ below was wonderful. We were flying over the skyscrapers of Manhattan Is _ _ _ _ _ . I cheered up suddenly. I knew I was going to enjoy my holiday.

Now write a short story called Holiday Adventure.

Silent letters crossword

Choose from these words:

half	knife	iron
know	foreign	comb
island	answer	climb
wrap	knee	bombs
reign	scene	numb

Clues across

1 We use a _ _ _ _ _ to cut bread.

3 We are going on a camping holiday at _ _ _ _ term.

5 When your father asks you a question you should always _ _ _ _ _ _ him.

7 My mother likes to _ _ _ _ my sandwiches in silver foil to keep them fresh.

8 I fell off my bike and grazed my _ _ _ _ .

11 The English Navy defeated the Spanish Armada in 1588, during the _ _ _ _ _ of Queen Elizabeth I.

13 I have to _ _ _ _ my hair thoroughly because it is long and curly.

14 During the Second World War many _ _ _ _ _ were dropped on London.

Clues down

1 You should always revise for an exam so that you _ _ _ _ the answers to the questions.

2 Jamaica is an _ _ _ _ _ _ in the West Indies.

4 I have a new stamp album and many _ _ _ _ _ _ _ stamps.

6 I had a small part in the school play and was only in the first _ _ _ _ _ .

9 We have to _ _ _ _ _ a ladder to get into our loft.

10 When your fingers are cold and you can't feel them we say they are _ _ _ _ _ .

12 I always _ _ _ _ my own shirts as my mother goes to work all day.

au (1)*

*Say the **au** like the **or** in **for**. In the second column the **gh** is silent.*

1	2	3	4	5
audience	caught	cause	haunt	caution
August	taught	pause	haunted	cautious
autumn	daughter	applause	launch	astronaut
author	slaughter	applaud	launderette	exhausted
authority	naughty	fraud	laundry	exhaust
autograph		haul	sauce	dinosaur
automatic		Paul	saucer	
automobile			saucepan	restaurant

A   What message told the American generals that the enemy was defeated?

 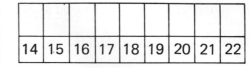

| 1 | 2 | 3 | | 4 | 5 | 6 | 7 | 8 | 9 | 10 | 11 | | 12 | 13 | | 14 | 15 | 16 | 17 | 18 | 19 | 20 | 21 | 22 |

1   If a cup generally stands on a saucer, write **T**; if it doesn't, write **H**.

2   If an astronaut is a traveller in the desert, write **a**;
    if he or she is a traveller in space, write **h**.

3   If the word exhausted means very tired, write **e**;
    if it doesn't, write **s**.

4   If the exhaust is the waste fumes from a car, write **a**;
    if it isn't, write **d**.

5   If an author is a man or woman who writes books, write **u**;
    if not, write **a**.

6   If the word haul means the entrance passage of a house, write **t**;
    if it means pull or drag, write **d**.

7   If the season of autumn comes after spring, write **g**;
    if it comes after summer, write **i**.

8   If the word caution warns you to take care, write **e**;
    if it doesn't, write **h**.

9   If a dinosaur is an unhappy man in a restaurant, write **t**;
    if it is a prehistoric animal, write **n** .

continued on page P2

continued from page P1

10	If a king or queen's daughter is called a princess, write **c**; if she isn't, write **o**.
11	If a break made in speaking or reading is called a pause, write **e**; if it isn't, write **o**.
12	If a haunted house is a house where horses are stabled, write **r**; if it is a house which is often visited by ghosts, write **i**.
13	If the word caught rhymes with the word taught, write **s**; if it doesn't, write **n**.
14	If you usually boil milk in a saucepan, write **e**; if you usually boil milk in a frying-pan, write **t**.
15	If you applaud when you don't like a performance, write **e**; if you applaud when you do like a performance, write **x**.
16	If a restaurant is a place where meals may be had, write **h**; if it isn't, write **l**.
17	If an automobile means the same as a car, write **a**; if it doesn't, write **e**.
18	If the month of August comes after July and before September, write **u**; if it doesn't, write **p**.
19	If an audience is a group of listeners or spectators, write **s**; if it isn't, write **h**.
20	If the word naughty means well behaved, write **o**; if it means badly behaved or disobedient, write **t**.
21	The word launch has many meanings. If one meaning is a motor boat for passengers, write **e**; if it isn't, write **n**.
22	If a launderette is a small patch of grass, write **e**; if it is a self-service laundry, write **d**.

B   *Put each word in a sentence: (1) restaurant   (2) audience   (3) caught   (4) automatic.*

....

....

....

....

au crossword

Choose from these words:

author	audience
taught	daughter
restaurant	haul
August	haunt
caught	naughty
autumn	launch
	saucer
laugh	
	aunt

Clues across

1 At the end of the pop concert the _ _ _ _ _ _ _ _ applauded loudly.

5 My father _ _ _ _ _ _ me how to play tennis.

7 When I went fishing I _ _ _ _ _ _ a large pike.

8 We saw the boat get stuck on the rocks and we helped to _ _ _ _ it off.

10 My father took us for a meal in an Indian _ _ _ _ _ _ _ _ _ _ .

11 The eighth month of the year is _ _ _ _ _ _ .

12 I always use a mug because I can't be bothered with a cup and _ _ _ _ _ _ .

13 The season which comes after summer is _ _ _ _ _ _ .

14 The Americans were going to _ _ _ _ _ _ a rocket in the second stage of their space project.

Clues down

1 Charles Dickens was the _ _ _ _ _ _ of *A Christmas Carol.*

2 My sister was disappointed when she had a son because she wanted a _ _ _ _ _ _ _ _ .

3 The clown at the circus made us _ _ _ _ _ _ .

4 Your mother's or father's sister is your _ _ _ _ .

6 The ghost of Anne Boleyn is supposed to _ _ _ _ _ Hampton Court Palace.

9 My mother said she felt exhausted because my baby brother had been _ _ _ _ _ _ _ _ all day.

qu (1)*

Say the qu as kw in these words.			Say the qu as k in these words.
1	**2**	**3**	**4**
quack	qualify	earthquake	cheque
queen	qualifications	inquire	antique
queer	quality	inquiries	technique
quench	quantity	equator	quay
question	quarrel	equipment	queue
quick		liquid	conquer
quiet	equal	request	mosquito
quite	quarter	require	
quilt	aquarium	inquisitive	
quiz		frequently	

A   Which two words are the Secret Service's password for this week?

 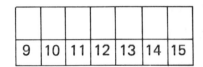

1   If an earthquake is a shaking of the earth's surface, write **q**; if it isn't, write **s**.

2   If there are two quarters in one half, write **u**; if there aren't, write **t**.

3   If the word equal means more than, write **l**; if it means has the same value as, write **e**.

4   If an aquarium is a tank for keeping live fish, write **s**; if it isn't, write **u**.

5   When you frequently go to the pictures, you go often. If this statement is true, write **t**; if it is false, write **p**.

6   If the opposite of liquid is solid, write **i**; if it isn't, write **o**.

7   If a quilt is another name for a quarrel, write **u**; if it is a padded bed-cover, write **o**.

continued on page P5

qu (2)*

continued from page P4

8	When a bus stop is a request stop you must put out your hand to ask the driver to stop. If this statement is true, write **n**; if it is false, write **o**.
9	If the region on or near the equator is cold, write **r**; if it is hot, write **q**.
10	If the word quiet means the same as the word quite, write **s**; if it doesn't, write **u**.
11	If a quiz is a test of knowledge, mostly as a form of entertainment, write **i**; if it isn't, write **a**.
12	If you need qualifications to be a mechanical engineer, write **e**; if you don't need any qualifications, write **i**.
13	To get a cheque book you must pay some money into a bank and open a bank account. If this statement is true, write **t**; if it is false, write **m**.
14	If you can open a door with a quay, write **n**; if you can't, write **l**.
15	If a queue is a line of people waiting for something, write **y**; if it isn't, write **l**.

B   Put each word in a sentence:
(1) quick   (2) quiet   (3) quite   (4) question   (5) quarrel   (6) equal   (7) quarter.

....

....

....

....

....

....

....

....

....

....

....

squ; say **skw***

1	2	3	4
squabble	squat	square	squint
squad	squatter	squeak	squirt
squadron		squeal	squirm
squash	squaw	squeeze	squirrel
	squawk		

A	What am I?	
	clues	answers
1	I am the wife of an American Indian.	....
2	I am a small animal with a busy tail. I eat nuts and like to climb trees.	....
3	I mean to quarrel.	....
4	I mean to crush or squeeze flat. I am also a drink made of crushed fruit — like orange	....
5	I am a part of an airforce or fleet.	....

B	Complete each sentence by putting the words at the side in the right order.	
1	Some people moved into the empty flat next to ours without permission. My mother .... and didn't have a home of their own.	said squatters they were
2	'Why do you always .... out of the syringe before you give me an injection?' I asked the nurse. 'It's to make sure that there isn't any air in the liquid,' she explained, 'because air injected into the blood can kill.'	some of squirt the liquid
3	My mother was in the parrot house at the zoo when a parrot .... She jumped, her glasses fell off and she stepped on them, squashing them flat.	squawk. gave loud a

C	Put each word in a sentence: (1) square (2) squeeze (3) squeak.
	....

tion; say sh'n (1)

Split each word into syllables (parts).

2 syllables	3 syllables	
1 action nation station caution fraction fiction section question	**2** attention invention direction collection election objection correction exception	**3** addition condition position prescription instructions solution

Complete each sentence by putting the words at the side in the right order.

1	Trains for Brighton	from Victoria	station. leave
2	I had a very good	toy collection	soldiers. of
3	After the teacher had marked our work we had	corrections. do	to our
4	After school I like looking at the	programme Nationwide	on television.
5	I hesitated for a .... before I dived off the top board.	second a	of fraction
6	The new James Bond film has plenty	of action	it. in
7	I got told off for not paying	in the lesson.	attention Maths
8	I gained fourth	class the position	exams. in
9	I was told to look in .... the library for the story of Oliver Twist.	fiction the	of section
10	When I was in the first year I couldn't do the	addition Maths.	in questions

tion; say **sh'n** (2)

Split each word into syllables (parts).

When **a** *comes before* **tion** *it has a long vowel sound* ā.

When **i** *comes before* **tion** *it has a short vowel sound* ĭ.

4 syllables		5 syllables
1	**2**	**3**
education	application	examination
population	navigation	civilisation
circulation	information	association
occupation	exploration	organisation
reputation	exhibition	multiplication
situation	composition	qualifications
conversation	dictionary	nationality
operation		

There are many more words that end in **tion**. Can you think of any?

Finish each sentence then read your sentences to the rest of your group.

1 The teacher said, 'You must learn all your multiplication tables because ....
....

2 I think education is ....
....

3 My .... examination was ....
....

4 I looked in the 'Situations Vacant' column of the newspaper and ....
....

5 The exhibition ....
....

6 I had a very interesting conversation ....
....

7 The word population means ....
....

8 I bought a dictionary because ....
....

9 The .... has a .... reputation because ....
....

tion

A *Complete the words in the story.*

Choose from these words:

objections	prescription	operation	instructions	action
conversation	circulation	condition	reputation	

JUST IN TIME

When I arrived home from school I flopped into a chair and flung my homework on the table.

'No sleeping yet.' My mother jogged the chair. 'Let's have some _ _ _ _ _ _ .'

'Oh Mum, I can't move,' I protested weakly.

'No o _ _ _ _ _ _ _ _ _ now, you'll have to get your father's medicine from the chemists'. Here's the p _ _ _ _ _ _ _ _ _ _ _ . Go on, it won't take long. He needs it tonight, that o _ _ _ _ _ _ _ left him very weak and these new pills help the c _ _ _ _ _ _ _ _ _ of the blood.'

She thrust the p _ _ _ _ _ _ _ _ _ _ _ into my hand. I examined it carefully.

'Dreadful writing! Do you think the chemist will be able to read the name of the medicine and the i _ _ _ _ _ _ _ _ _ _ _ ?' I said.

'This c _ _ _ _ _ _ _ _ _ _ _ is getting us nowhere,' Mum replied. 'Never mind the writing, just hurry up and get to the chemist's before it closes.'

'Right,' I said and hurried out. 'Poor Dad,' I thought, 'that o _ _ _ _ _ _ _ _ certainly left him very weak. Still, the hospital has a good r _ _ _ _ _ _ _ _ _ . I'm sure his c _ _ _ _ _ _ _ will improve.'

I arrived at the chemist's just before it closed. 'Just in time. That was a stroke of luck,' I said to myself as I handed in Dad's p _ _ _ _ _ _ _ _ _ _ _ .

B *Put each word in a sentence: (1) position (2) direction (3) information.*

....

....

....

....

tion crossword

Choose from these words

- application
- exhibition
- position
- nation
- examination
- action
- attention
- direction
- conversation
- dictionary
- fiction
- caution

Clues across

1 A request. You fill in one of these forms when you apply for a job.

7 A public display of things like paintings, furniture, boats, etc.

8 Something imagined. A made-up story is called this.

10 People in any one country who are under the same government.

11 Talk between two or more people.

Clues down

1 Careful listening.

2 Movement. (Out of _ _ _ _ _ _ means not working properly.)

3 (a) A test of knowledge.   (b) A careful inspection.

4 Instruction on how to do something.

5 A book giving the spellings and meanings of words.

6 The place of something. I altered the _ _ _ _ _ _ _ _ of my bed.

9 A warning; pay attention to safety.

sion and ssion; say sh'n and zh'n*

	Say zh'n			Say sh'n	
1		**2**	**3**		**4**
collision		explosion	pension		emulsion
decision		invasion	mansion		discussion
vision		occasion	mission		expression
revision		occasionally	admission		possession
division		diversion	permission		procession
television		confusion	expansion		comprehension

Complete the words in these sentences. Choose from the words that are underlined.

1   I saw the Lord Mayor's Pr _ _ _ _ _ _ _ _   on t _ _ _ _ _ _ _ _ _ _ .

    It was a very grand o _ _ _ _ _ _ _ .

2   When my grandmother gets her pen _ _ _ _ she oc _ _ _ _ _ _ _ _ ly gives me some

    money, and if my mother gives me per _ _ _ _ _ _ _ I go roller skating.

3   Our Science teacher said that a sudden expa _ _ _ _ _ of gas

    causes an expl _ _ _ _ _ .

4   The motorist didn't see the di _ _ _ _ _ _ _ sign. He drove down a one-way

    street and had a col _ _ _ _ _ _ with a bus.

5   Our English teacher said that it was difficult to do re _ _ _ _ _ _ for

    the comp _ _ _ _ _ _ _ _ _ exam.

6   M.I.6 employs secret agents who are sent out on

    dangerous m _ _ _ _ _ _ s.

7   I asked my parents what colour I could paint my bedroom walls.

    They said it was my de _ _ _ _ _ _ , so I used orange em _ _ _ _ _ _ .

8   Germany's in _ _ _ _ _ _ of Poland in 1939 was the start of the

    Second World War.

9   The price of ad _ _ _ _ _ _ _ to the cinema is

    now very high.

10 In our English lesson we had a very interesting dis _ _ _ _ _ _ _ _

    about school uniform.

sion crossword

Choose from these words:

- explosion
- expression
- diversion
- collision
- mission
- invasion
- decision
- pension
- procession
- mansion
- vision

Clues across

1 I always know when my father is angry by the _ _ _ _ _ _ _ _ _ _ on his face.

5 When two cars collide they are said to be in _ _ _ _ _ _ _ _ _ .

6 When you retire you receive an old age _ _ _ _ _ _ _ .

9 Another name for a very large house is a _ _ _ _ _ _ _ .

8 When an army invades a foreign country we talk about an _ _ _ _ _ _ _ _ .

10 I can never decide what to do because I am very bad at making a _ _ _ _ _ _ _ _ .

Clues down

1 When a bomb explodes there is an _ _ _ _ _ _ _ _ _ .

2 In a carnival there is a _ _ _ _ _ _ _ _ _ _ of people and floats along the road.

3 When a road is being mended traffic is sometimes diverted along another road. This is called a _ _ _ _ _ _ _ _ .

4 James Bond had a very dangerous _ _ _ _ _ _ _ in his last film.

7 When you take a driving test the examiner tests your _ _ _ _ _ _ _ .

ph

Say the **ph** like the **f** in **fat**.			
1	**2**	**3**	**4**
alphabet	graph	phantom	dolphin
elephant	autograph	physical	sphere
telephone	paragraph	physics	atmosphere
nephew	telegraph	pharmacy	typhoon
orphan	photograph	pharaoh	amphibian
Geography	photography	sapphire	prophet
hyphen			decipher

What am I?

	clues	answers
1	I am another name for a ghost.	....
2	I am another name for a chemist's shop where you can have your prescriptions made up.	....
3	I am the title of the ancient rulers of Egypt.	....
4	I am a young person whose parents are dead.	....
5	I am the name for the air that surrounds the earth.	....
6	I am a diagram that shows facts and figures by means of a line on squared paper.	....
7	I am your brother's or sister's son.	....
8	I am a study of the earth's surface, climate, population, etc.	....
9	I am a very violent storm. I occur mainly in the China Sea.	....
10	I am the name of the small sign which joins these words: juke-box, ice-cream, mother-in-law.	....
11	I am a picture taken by a camera.	....
12	I am an animal that can live on land or in water. I am also an aeroplane or tank that can operate on land or water.	....

ph crossword

Choose from these words:

orphan	photography
prophet	elephant
nephew	telephone
alphabet	paragraphs
graph	physical
hyphen	

Clues across

1 I like taking photographs so I will choose the

_ _ _ _ _ _ _ _ _ _ _

option in the fourth year.

3 My friend has been an

_ _ _ _ _ _ since he was three, when his parents died in a car crash.

5 The teacher taught us how to show facts and figures by means of a line on squared paper. 'This is called a _ _ _ _ _ ,' he said.

8 When I went to the circus I saw an _ _ _ _ _ _ _ _ lift someone onto his back with his trunk.

9 The first electric _ _ _ _ _ _ _ _ _ was made in 1876 by Alexander Graham Bell.

10 Our English teacher reminded us that our compositions had to be arranged in

_ _ _ _ _ _ _ _ _ _ .

Clues down

1 Elijah was an Old Testament _ _ _ _ _ _ _ .

2 P.E. means _ _ _ _ _ _ _ _ education.

4 There are 26 letters in the _ _ _ _ _ _ _ _ .

6 James is my brother's son so he is my _ _ _ _ _ _ .

7 If you put a _ _ _ _ _ _ between juke and box you make the word juke-box.

ought (**ort**) and ough (ō)*

Say the **ought** like the **ort** in port.		Say the **ough** like the ō in home.	
1 ought, bought, brought	**2** fought, thought, nought	**3** dough, doughnuts	**4** though, although

---

A   Complete the words with spaces. Choose from the words above.

THE DOUGHNUT DISASTER

'You o _ _ _ _ to make some nice jam d _ _ _ _ _ _ _ _ ,' Mum said suddenly.

'I b _ _ _ _ _ some flour yesterday.'

I looked up. She was leafing through her recipe books; one of her favourite occupations.

'I th _ _ _ _ _ Aunt June borrowed the baking tray,' I said.

'You don't need a baking tray. Anyway, I b _ _ _ _ _ _ our tray home yesterday. June b _ _ _ _ _ one for herself on Saturday.'

I looked at the recipe. 'It looks easy. I'll try it this afternoon.'

Later I made the d _ _ _ _ and left it to double its size. After one and a half hours I took the d _ _ _ _ out of the bowl and kneaded it thoroughly. I formed it into balls, put in the jam and cooked them in hot fat for eight minutes.

A _ _ _ _ _ _ _ I followed the instructions very carefully the d _ _ _ _ _ _ _ _ still tasted as t _ _ _ _ _ _ I had used concrete instead of flour! Next time I'll buy them.

B   Put each word in a sentence: (1) fought   (2) ought   (3) bought   (4) although.

....

....

....

....

....

....

our

Say the **our** like the **er** in **butter**.			Say the **our** like the **er** in **her**.
1 colour harbour labour neighbour	**2** armour humour rumour honour	**3** favour flavour behaviour	**4** journey journalist

A   Complete the words with spaces. Choose from the words above.

1   My n _ _ _ _ _ _ _ _ is a j _ _ _ _ _ _ _ _ _ _ on the Sun newspaper.

2   I went on a car j _ _ _ _ _ _ to Portsmouth h _ _ _ _ _ _ to watch the

c _ _ _ _ _ ful sailing boats.

3   Although John's b _ _ _ _ _ _ _ _ in class was not very good he had a keen sense of

hu _ _ _ _ and never seemed to get into trouble.

4   In the Middle Ages both the knights and their horses used to wear a _ _ _ _ _

in battle. It was considered an h _ _ _ _ _ to be asked to fight for your

king or queen.

5   There is a r _ _ _ _ _ going about the school that our Geography teacher has

resigned. (I know this is untrue because he is my aunt's n _ _ _ _ _ _ _ _ and she

told me that he is away because he is ill.)

6   Another word for hard work is l _ _ _ _ _ _ .

7   My mother said, 'Do me a f _ _ _ _ _ and tell me if the fl _ _ _ _ _ of the cake

is all right or if it needs more chocolate.

B   Put each word in a sentence: (1) colour   (2) neighbour   (3) journey.

....

....

....

ou saying o͞o and o͝o

Say the **ou** *like the* **oo** *in* **moon**.		Say the **ou** *like the* **oo** *in* **book**.
soup group coupon route	youth through tourist tour	could would should

Choose from the words that are underlined in the columns above, and these words:

rock   rude   shout   space   rest

Clues across

1   These are people who make tours or who travel for pleasure.

5   This is a ticket or form which entitles the holder to some payment or service. It is also an entry form for a competition.

8   This word means a number of persons or things together.

11   This is the past tense of 'can'.

12   This word has many meanings. One meaning is to be still and quiet and not involved in any activity. (Find out the other meanings.)

Clues down

1   This word has many meanings. One meaning is to pass from one end to the other: I walked _ _ _ _ _ _ _ the village.

2   This means (a) a solid stone, (b) to move gently to and fro. It is also a sweet that is sold mostly at the seaside.

3   This is a liquid food made by boiling vegetables or meat.

4   This means to call loudly.

6   This word means ways to get to a place: There are many different _ _ _ _ _ _ to Spain.

7   One meaning of this word is the region beyond the earth's atmosphere.

9   This means a young man.

10   One meaning of this word is ill mannered.

ou saying ŭ and ough saying ŭff*

Learn how to read and spell all these words.		
Say the **ou** *like the* **u** *in* **but**.		Say the **ough** *like the* **uff** *in* **puff**.
1	**2**	**3**
country	double	enough
couple	trouble	rough
courage	touch	tough
cousin	young	
		cough

The Second World War lasted from September 1939 to September 1945.

On D-Day, 6th June 1944, British, American and Canadian troops crossed the Channel and invaded Normandy in northern France.

After winning control of Normandy from the Germans the British moved through Belgium and Holland towards Germany. The Americans and Canadians moved on to Paris which they freed from the Germans on 24th August 1944.

The missing words in the letter below are in code. Find out what they are.

The code:

a	b	c	d	e	f	g	h	i	j	k	l	m	n	o	p	q	r	s	t	u	v	w	x	y	z
1	2	3	4	5	6	7	8	9	10	11	12	13	14	15	16	17	18	19	20	21	22	23	24	25	26

A LETTER HOME

Somewhere near Paris,
22nd August, 1944.

Dear Mum and Dad

The going is .... but we are not having any ....
18 15 21 7 8   20 18 15 21 2 12 5

passing through the .... villages. There is .... food as
3 15 21 14 20 18 25   5 14 15 21 7 8

we now have .... rations. .... is our motto and the
4 15 21 2 12 5   3 15 21 18 1 7 5

men are .... and .... enough to overcome the hardships.
20 15 21 7 8   25 15 21 14 7

The captain's .... trod on a land mine yesterday. You only
3 15 21 19 9 14

have to .... these mines to be blown to pieces. Poor man!
20 15 21 3 8

We are now only a .... of miles from Paris which we will
3 15 21 16 12 5

enter tomorrow or the next day. I hope this terrible war will soon be over.

Love,
Tony

ous and ious

Say ous *as* ŭs *and* ious *as* ĭŭs.				
ous			**ious**	
1 famous nervous jealous	**2** dangerous generous treacherous	**3** tremendous enormous poisonous marvellous	**4** serious curious furious various	**5** mysterious obvious previous anxious

Complete each sentence by putting the words at the side in the right order.

1	It is dangerous to eat mushrooms you pick in the country because	may be	they poisonous.
2	There are .... which look just like mushrooms but are poisonous to eat.	fungus various	types of
3	I have a marvellous job in a bank which I enjoy immensely. I had to .... because my boss was always shouting and he made me very nervous.	previous job	my leave
4	My dog is .... When the cat is sitting on my lap the dog always tries to push him off.	my of very cat. jealous	
5	My father bought .... a Great Dane. My mother was furious. She said he was too big for our small house.	enormous called	an dog
6	The Beatles were a famous singing group. They made a .... from their records.	of amount	tremendous money
7	My father is going into hospital to	a serious	have operation.
8	My aunt is a very generous person. Two days before my birthday she gave me a parcel. I was .... it contained but I didn't open it until my birthday. It was a portable radio.	what know	curious to
9	The boatman told us not to go near the rocks. 'Although they look .... and have claimed many lives,' he said.	harmless treacherous	are they

cial and cious*

Say the **ci** *as* **sh.**			
cial (sh'l)		**cious** (shŭs)	
1 social special specialist	**2** especially artificial official	**3** delicious suspicious vicious	**4** precious conscious unconscious ferocious

---

A *From the words listed above choose the word that fits the meaning. Use your dictionary.*

meaning	word
1 I mean fierce or savage.	....
2 I mean something that is not real or natural.	....
3 One of my meanings is a person in charge of public affairs.	....
4 I am a person who makes a study of one particular thing.	....
5 I mean aware of what one is doing or thinking.	....
6 I mean priceless or valuable.	....
7 I am another word for spiteful or wicked.	....
8 I mean very pleasing, especially to eat.	....
9 I mean suspecting something.	....

B *In these sentences pair the best adjective with the noun.*

Choose from these adjectives:

delicious   unconscious   special   artificial   ferocious   social

1 The Capri restaurant always serves .... meals.

2 The man walked in a strange way because he had an .... leg.

3 Our local butcher has bought a .... Alsatian dog to guard his meat store.

4 My father belongs to his firm's .... club.

5 The doctor tried to revive the .... man.

6 I am going to the zoo as a .... birthday treat.

cian (sh'n)

Say the ci as sh.

*When you see **cian** at the end of a word, you know it is the name of a person who practises a particular job or skill. The first part of the word gives you a clue about the job.*

1	2	3	4
musician electrician	optician politician	technician physician	magician beautician

A What am I?

clues	answers
1 I am skilled in magic.	....
2 I am skilled in dealing with electricity or electrical equipment.	....
3 I am skilled in the practice of music.	....
4 I am a doctor of medicine. I specialise in medical treatment.	....
5 I make or sell glasses (spectacles).	....
6 I take part in politics as a profession.	....
7 I am skilled in using my technical knowledge.	....
8 I am a beauty specialist.	....

B Put each word in a sentence: (1) electrician (2) optician (3) musician (4) beautician.

....

....

....

....

....

....

....

....

....